Discovery

and the

Capitalist

Process

Discovery

and the

Capitalist

Process

Israel M. Kirzner

The University of
Chicago Press
Chicago & London

ISRAEL M. KIRZNER is professor of
economics at New York University. He
is the author of *Competition and
Entrepreneurship* and *Perception,
Opportunity, and Profit,* both published
by the University of Chicago Press.

THE UNIVERSITY OF CHICAGO PRESS,
CHICAGO 60637
THE UNIVERSITY OF CHICAGO PRESS,
LTD., LONDON

94 93 92 91 90 89 88 87 86 85   54321

Library of Congress Cataloging in Publication Data

Kirzner, Israel M.
Discovery and the capitalist process.

Contents: Entrepreneurship, economics, and
economists—The primacy of entrepreneurial discovery—
Uncertainty, discovery, and human action—[etc.]
Bibliography: p.
Includes index.
1. Entrepreneur—Addresses, essays, lectures.
2. Capitalism—Addresses, essays, lectures.
3. Uncertainty—Addresses, essays, lectures.   4. Learning
by discovery—Addresses, essays, lectures.   I. Title.
HB615.K57   1985   338'.04   85-5799
ISBN 0-226-43777-9

B'Ezras Hashem

To Alexander A. Katz
and Bernard Redner
with deepest gratitude for years
of unforgettable kindness

Contents

Preface

Capitalism, it is evident, resides in the eye of the beholder. What for some appears as institutionalized exploitation, or fraud, or chaos, or all of these together is seen by others as a well-oiled, efficient social engine working smoothly and flawlessly to achieve spectacular growth, prosperity, and economic justice. These diverse evaluative perspectives on the free enterprise economy— and the innumerable other perspectives that lie between these poles—are likely, in turn, to reflect different positive theories of how capitalism works. For economists the task of arriving at an understanding of the market system has always ranked as a central responsibility of their discipline. It is not surprising, therefore, that the multiplicity of schools of economic thought has spawned a corresponding variety of ways of "seeing" capitalism. What unites the seven papers offered in this volume is a particular positive vision of capitalism—absorbed from the "Austrian" tradition in modern economic thought— that they express. The papers explore this vision and probe some of its normative and policy implications.

These essays see market capitalism not simply as a set of institutions governing exchanges, not as a set of activities or prices (or both) continuously reflecting with attained accuracy the changing patterns of relative supply and demand, but as an ongoing *process of creative discovery*. What one witnesses in a market economy, at any point in time, are nothing but attempts by market participants to take advantage of newly discovered or created possibilities. In the course of seeking to implement *these* plans, market participants notice, again, *further* market possibilities that had hitherto escaped attention. And so on. The process is kept continuously boiling by the incessant injection of unexpected changes and surprises. The process of creative discovery is never completed, nor is it ever arrested.

This view of the market constitutes a chain of understanding made up of three links. The first link was forged by Ludwig von Mises in seeing the market as an *entrepreneurial* process—a never-ending series of profit-motivated disequilibrium moves, tending continually in the direction of improved coordination, but ceaselessly buffeted by exogenous surprises. The second link was fashioned by Friedrich Hayek in his pioneering insights into the nature of equilibrating market processes. Hayek showed how any such process is to be understood as a process of *learning*, during which market participants learn mutually to adjust their activities so as to dovetail better and better with the other dispersed bits of knowledge scattered throughout the market, concerning individual preferences and concerning resource availabilities. The third link emerges, as will be seen in these papers, when we recognize that entrepreneurial activities that win profits are indeed creative acts of *discovery*. Thus the entrepreneurial process associated with any given (endogenous or exogenous) surprise can be perceived as a spontaneous, orderly process of undeliberate learning—one that would cease only if relevant mutual knowledge were complete.

Chapter 1 shows—against the shifting background of the modern history of economic thought—how this way of seeing the market process enables one to steer a careful middle path between two prevalent, and unhelpfully extreme, views concerning the nature of entrepreneurship in markets. Chapter 2 develops some of the basic elements that enter into my "discovery process" view of capitalism and comments on the limited scope for such discovery processes in alternative systems of social economic organization. Chapter 3 probes some of the subtleties involved in seeing entrepreneurial activity as grappling with the *uncertainty* that is inescapably bound up with the discovery view of capitalism. Chapter 4 applies my view of capitalism to a consideration of how capitalist growth and development are to be seen as integral aspects of the very same entrepreneurial process of creative discovery. Chapters 5 and 6 relate this view of the capitalist process to certain key aspects of public policy. I point out in chapter 5 that this view of the capitalist process has profound implications for understanding how alternative patterns of taxation may impinge on the system. Chapter 6 offers, from the perspective of the "discovery view," an unorthodox critique of economic regulation, pointing out the danger that regulation not only may (as standard theory has shown) distort incentives and allocate resources inefficiently, but may significantly stunt the discovery process that constitutes the heart of the system. Finally, chapter 7 points out how my view of capitalism as a process of discovery sharply affects our ability to envision the long-run future of the market economy. The discussion takes notice of the shortsightedness of those who, not recognizing the open-ended character of entrepreneurial discovery, repeatedly fall into the trap of forecasting the future against the background of *today's* expectations rather than against the unknowable background of tomorrow's discoveries.

A word of apology is due for a certain degree of unavoidable repetition. Each of these papers was prepared for a different occasion. A number of them spell out certain key elements of the "capitalism as discovery process view" that may have already been encountered in the other papers. This slim volume has no pretensions about being a systematic treatise on its theme. It is instead, a collection of essays published in the course of the years during which this theme crystallized. It was thought that at least part of the value of these essays may consist in their retaining the form in which they emerged during these gestative years. Without doing substantial violence to these papers as originally published, there was simply no way to eliminate the repetition they do contain.

I am indebted to many friends and colleagues in regard to the papers in this book. The Sarah Scaife Foundation has supported the research that, over a period of years, led to this volume. Richard M. Larry's vision and his appreciation for the insights this research has pursued call for special and grateful recognition. A number of the papers included here owe their genesis, at least in part, to the intellectual entrepreneurship of several perceptive scholars. In this regard I am deeply grateful to Arthur Seldon (whose inspired prodding resulted in chapter 2), Calvin Kent (who filled a similarly wholesome role in regard to chapter 4), Dwight Lee (and also David Theroux and Charles Baird) in regard to chapter 5, and Peter Aranson (who most imaginatively sparked the idea that eventually resulted in chapter 6). The late Jules Backman, colleague and friend for many years, was instrumental in the emergence of chapter 7.

Many of the ideas in this book have been discussed with great vigor for many semesters around the Austrian Economics Colloquium table at New York University. I recall with pleasure and gratitude the valuable comments of Ludwig Lachmann, Gerald O'Driscoll, Mario Rizzo, Lawrence White, Richard Ebeling, and Roger Garrison. To these scholars, and to the many student colloquium participants over the years, I am deeply grateful. Others to whom I feel a significant debt of gratitude for their direct or indirect help in regard to this volume include George Pearson, Leonard Liggio, Walter Grinder, Neil McLeod, Ken Templeton, Roy Childs, and Greg Lindsay.

Acknowledgments

Six of the papers in this volume have already appeared in earlier publications. Permission to republish these papers here is most gratefully acknowledged by the author and the publisher. Thanks are due, specifically, to the following:

The Institute of Economic Affairs, London, for permission to republish chapter 2. This paper was presented at an Institute Colloquium held in London in October 1979 and was first published in Israel Kirzner et al., *The Prime Mover of Progress: The Entrepreneur in Capitalism and Socialism*, ed. A. Seldon (1980).

Lexington Books, D. C. Heath and Company, for permission to republish chapters 3 and 4. Chapter 3 was first published in I. M. Kirzner, ed., *Method, Process, and Austrian Economics: Essays in Honor of Ludwig von Mises* (1982). Chapter 4 was first published in Calvin A. Kent, ed., *The Environment for Entrepreneurship* (1984).

The Pacific Institute for Public Policy Research, for permission to republish chapter 5, first published in Dwight R. Lee, ed., *Taxation and Capital Markets* (1985).

The Law and Economics Center, University of Miami, for permission to republish chapter 6, which first appeared as an Occasional Paper of the center, 1979.

The Macmillan Publishing Company, for permission to republish chapter 7, which first appeared in Jules A. Backman, ed., *Entrepreneurship and the Outlook for America* (1983).

ONE

Entrepreneurship, Economics, and Economists

During the past two hundred years of history of economic thought, four separate stages can be distinguished in respect to the significance economists attach to the entrepreneurial role in the market economy.

As is well known, the classical economists (with some notable exceptions such as J. B. Say, who continued the French tradition begun by Cantillon) did not recognize an entrepreneurial function distinct from that of the capitalist. For the classical economists "profit" meant the income share received by the capitalist, with no attempt made to distinguish pure interest separately from (what we would today call) pure entrepreneurial profit.[1] In the classical schema, they sought to understand the important characteristics of the capitalist economy within a framework that ignored the entrepreneurial role.

In the decades following the marginalist revolution, a vigorous literature emerged in which the entrepreneurial role was thoroughly discussed. During the 1880s and subsequently, entrepreneurship and entrepreneurial profit were the subject of doctoral dissertations and journal articles,[2] including contributions by some leading neoclassical theorists. An American economist prominent at the turn of the century, F. B. Hawley, made this topic his lifework. And of course the second decade of the present century saw the fully elaborated theories of entrepreneurship developed by Schumpeter and by Knight. The first half-century of neoclassical ascendancy was a period in which the entrepreneurial role was identified and its subtleties and elusiveness thoroughly, if perhaps not quite definitively, explored.

But the half-century that began about 1920, a half-century during which modern microeconomic theory attained a significantly higher standard of sophistication, saw economists paying scarcely any attention at all to analyzing the ways entrepreneurial activity affects the course of events in markets. To cite an often-quoted observation of Professor Baumol, the entrepreneur "virtually disappeared from the theoretical literature."[3]

The fourth stage to be identified has thus far endured for only a very few years—perhaps the session devoted to the entrepreneur in the December 1967 meetings of the American Economic Association can be taken as its beginning. During these past few years economists have rediscovered the entrepreneur, and the topic has been explored in conferences and books (including one book devoted to a history of economic thought on entrepreneurship).[4] Whether this flurry of activity has produced significant advances in economic understanding may not be universally agreed on, but certainly it must be recognized that the earlier modern tradition of neglect for the entrepreneurial role has, during this current stage, been decisively broken.

This opening chapter has two principal objectives. The first is to suggest an explanation for the rather surprising neglect of the entrepreneurial role during the half-century following 1920 and for the no less mysterious reappearance, in recent years, of the entrepreneur among the dramatis personae recognized by economic theory. The second, related objective will be to proceed, from the suggestions advanced in fulfilling the first objective, to consider some of the difficulties that surround contemporary attempts to reintegrate the entrepreneurial role into economic understanding. In a number of ways the ideas developed in this chapter will serve as a foundation for much that I will elaborate upon later.

The Appearance and the Disappearance of the Entrepreneurial Role

That the marginalist revolution brought in its train an awareness of the need for separate attention to the entrepreneur is not surprising. It was in the course of this revolution that economists came to view factor incomes no longer as shares of national output but as the revenues received in return for the sale, at market prices, of productive services (valued by the purchasing factor employers for their incremental contribution to output). As this way of seeing factor incomes was more thoroughly developed, it was only natural that the pure profits won by the energetic, daring, innovative entrepreneur were perceived to constitute an altogether different economic category. Pure profits, it came to be seen, are what remain after *all* factors of production have received their appropriate marginal-productivity rewards, rewards sufficient to elicit all the resource effort needed to deliver the relevant output. It was recognition of this circumstance that spurred economists at that time to search for what it was that entrepreneurs did that was not covered by the neoclassical marginalist view of production. It was here that economists debated the significance of change, of innovation, or of uncertainty.

But this very recognition by economists that entrepreneurial activity resists the marginalist's mode of analysis eventually caused the banishment of such activity from the theorist's purview. Such banishment had already been foreshadowed in Walras's treatment, where the entrepreneur was permitted neither to win any profits nor to suffer any losses. It is plausible to argue that as economic theory became more sophisticated, as marginal analysis and market equilibrium theory came to be more carefully and more fully articulated, the entrepreneur receded more and more from theoretical view. This seems to have been the result of two mutually reinforcing (if perhaps not wholly consistent) attitudes.

First, it seems probable that theorists came to see it as something like an analytical *virtue* to abstract from entrepreneurship. After all, it is the theorist's task to pierce the superficial veil of ever changing daily events in order to grasp the enduring underlying regularities upon which these ephemeral events are superimposed. An understanding of markets, the neoclassical economists came to believe, requires us to focus on the sets of optimizing decisions that can all be simultaneously accommodated. To the extent that at a given time entrepreneurial daring and innovation generate activities that cannot be so accommodated, they constitute phenomena that *obstruct* theoretical vision of that underlying equilibrium set of potential activities that is alone fully consistent with the basic data, consumer tastes, resource constraints, and available technology. From this perspective the theorist sees it as his responsibility *not* to permit his attention to be diverted (by concern with the theory-defying vagaries of adventurous, original entrepreneurs) from the deeper systematic regularities that lie waiting to be discerned.

Second, as the equilibrium perspective of neoclassical microeconomics became more and more dominant during this period, and particularly as Walrasian modes of thinking came to pervade that microeconomics since the 1930s, it became fashionable to treat the real world as if it were indeed close to equilibrium at all times. In other words, the neoclassical theorist fell, in effect, into the habit of considering markets to be fully coordinated, with entrepreneurs making neither profits nor losses (just as in the Walrasian system). From this point of view any apparent discrepancies between the real world and equilibrium conditions are more likely to be held to reflect complete adjustment to some overlooked real circumstances (overlooked, that is, by the applied theorist in his identification of the relevant conditions for equilibrium) than to be seen as evidence of disequilibrium. Once again the result was to withdraw analytical attention from phenomena that could not be fitted into the equilibrium mold.

The Rediscovery of the Entrepreneur

The two attitudes just identified as plausibly responsible for the failure of modern microeconomics since the 1920s to grapple with the entrepreneurial role seem to correspond to two separate reasons that possibly have contributed to the current rediscovery of that role by economists.

With the economics of general equilibrium fully developed by the 1970s, it was perhaps understandable that theorists began to turn their attention to facts that did not fit easily into the equilibrium mold. While it might have appeared an analytical virtue in earlier times to avoid concentrating on such entrepreneurially generated elements, it now became something of a theoretical challenge to do so. With general equilibrium theory considered settled territory, the analytical frontiers were seen, at least by some economists, to be situated in terrain characterized by entrepreneurial discovery, innovation, and bold speculation under uncertainty. The very irrelevance, for such activities, of traditional microeconomic tools only enhanced the challenge these frontiers offered to economic theory.

And again, other economists, growing impatient with the patently implausible assumption that the world is at all times in the neighborhood of equilibrium, began to focus their analytical curiosity on phenomena (such as entrepreneurial activity) that seem most blatantly to give the lie to that assumption. For such economists the technical sophistication that had characterized modern microeconomic theory came to be seen less as advanced virtuosity than as arid, formal exercises with less and less relevance for the real world. The study of entrepreneurship seemed called for not so much to extend the corpus of economic theory beyond its existing equilibrium scope as to come to grips with what began to appear as the glaring irrelevance of the corpus of received theory for the phenomena of the market around us.

We shall discover that these various insights hold some significance for the specific ways contemporary economists have variously sought to reintegrate the role of the entrepreneur into economic understanding. Let us pause to reflect on the many activities we associate with entrepreneurial behavior and upon what distinctive characteristics we may perhaps perceive as common to all of them.

Entrepreneurial Activities and the Essence of Entrepreneurship

The kinds of activities we associate with entrepreneurial vision and energy are varied and numerous. They include, certainly, forming new business ventures; introducing new products; initiating new techniques of production; altering prices (offers or bids) to meet or to forestall competitors; striking out in new territory to identify new markets for one's product; identifying new sources of finance; and streamlining internal patterns of organization.

What is remarkable is that economists have, over the past two and a half centuries, reached such a variety of conflicting conclusions concerning the essential character of such entrepreneurial activities.[5] For some writers entrepreneurial activities are simply a special kind of labor; for others what is distinctive about them is their innovative character, their ability to disrupt the status quo; for yet others it is their *speculative* aspect (i.e., their taking a position with respect to the *uncertain* future). Some economists saw the entrepreneur as *middleman*, as *arbitrageur*; others saw him as *leader*; others as *employer*. Some theorists found the essence of entrepreneurship in its *coordinating*, "gap-filling" role; others found it in the entrepreneur's deployment of superior *information*.

I have, over a number of years, found it useful to recognize the central role played by *alertness* of the entrepreneur. What is entrepreneurial about the activities listed at the beginning of this section is, in this view, that each reflects the decision maker's belief that he has discovered possibilities that both he and his actual or potential competitors had hitherto not seen. Such discoveries may reflect alertness to changed conditions or to overlooked possibilities. Scope for such alertness is afforded not only by unexploited opportunities offered by existing conditions but also, and especially so, by those to be created by future conditions. (In regard to opportunities to be created by future conditions, of course, "alertness" refers not to the ability to see what exists, but to the necessarily speculative ability to "see" into the future. In particular, such metaphorical "alertness" may consist in the vision to *create* something in the future.)[6] The crucial element in behavior expressing entrepreneurial alertness is that it expresses the decision maker's ability spontaneously to transcend an existing framework of perceived opportunities.

We turn now to observe how this "alertness" perspective on entrepreneurial behavior represents a "middle way" between two alternative ("extreme") modes of treating such behavior that have been discussed in the contemporary literature.

Two Extreme Views

The two "extreme" views that have been discussed point in diametrically opposite directions. The one view sees the entrepreneur as responding systematically and frictionlessly to the conditions of the market, with pure entrepreneurial profit the smoothly corresponding reward that these market conditions require and make possible. From this perspective entrepreneurship is "called forth" systematically, if not quite predictably, by these market conditions. I will call this (for reasons to be made appar-

ent shortly) the "neoclassical" view of the entrepreneur.
The second view sees entrepreneurship not as *responding
to* external market conditions, but as independently and
spontaneously *injecting* new elements *into* those conditions, in a manner totally unpredictable from and wholly
undetermined by existing circumstances. The "neoclassical" view is exemplified by the work of T. W.
Schultz; the opposite extreme view is associated with the
work of G. L. S. Shackle.

Schultz's view sees the entrepreneur[7] as performing
a needed service in the market—the service of reallocating resources under conditions of disequilibrium. This
service is valuable in definite ways, and there is therefore
a demand curve for it. The ability to provide this service
("the ability to deal with disequilibria") is scarce, and
there is a supply curve with respect to it. This service
therefore tends to command a market price that is, in
principle, implied by the relevant supply and demand
conditions. Notice that the quantity and varieties of entrepreneurial services performed, and also the size of pure
profit, are "determined" by these given supply and demand conditions. The level of pure entrepreneurial profit
seems to be adjusted through market competition, in this
view, so as to bring the supply of and the demand for entrepreneurial ability into mutual coordination. At any
given time, in other words, the "right" quantity of entrepreneurial services is forthcoming, that is, the "right"
quantity of the service of dealing with disequilibria is at
all times being appropriately deployed. Clearly the direction this Schultzian view of entrepreneurship is pointing
is one in which full coordination, in the relevant sense, is
always maintained by the market. The market is always
generating the correct volume of services needed to correct incorrect decisions. This direction, one fears, is likely
to lead to a neoclassical world whose full and continuous
equilibrium necessarily leaves the entrepreneur no scope
whatever for spontaneous innovative activity. This neoclassical approach has, it seems, merely squeezed the

real-world entrepreneur back into the neoclassical full-equilibrium box.

The alternative extreme approach, which I have associated with the work of G. L. S. Shackle, reflects a general impatience with neoclassical microeconomic theory and especially with the notion of individual choice that that theory employs. So far from being prepared to let the activities of the entrepreneur be subsumed under (indeed swallowed up by) the equilibrium calculus of supply and demand, Shackle's approach, in effect, sees the validity of the latter calculus as seriously compromised by the *universality* of what others might call entrepreneurial choice. Where the notion of choice employed in equilibrium theory sees decisions as determinate, mechanically generated by calculative reason operating upon the given objective conditions and the given preferences that make up the environment, Shackle emphasizes that choice is an "originative and imaginative art,"[8] in no sense an automatic response to given circumstances. The critique of received microeconomic theory implied in this perspective on choice recognizes that the systematic results of microeconomic theory depend upon our ability to abstract from the troublesome entrepreneurial, "originative" elements in the real world. But whereas this may have led earlier theorists to ignore these troublesome elements, and thus to neglect the role of the entrepreneur almost entirely it has led Shackle to quite different conclusions. For Shackle it is precisely these troublesome "entrepreneurial" features of human decision making that we *cannot*, in good conscience, filter out of our explanations. Thus this refusal to compress entrepreneurship within the equilibrium constraints of supply and demand theory has led not to the identification of a range of phenomena for which received microeconomic theory holds little relevance, but to serious questioning of the usefulness of that theory as a whole. Human choice is originative, "entrepreneurially" injecting new knowledge, new expectations, new imaginings, new dreams, into the existing situation. We must, Shackle therefore argues, reject the ambitious claims made by neoclassical economics to provide explanations of market phenomena that depend wholly on equilibrium configurations of maximizing decisions.

Clearly, these views of Schultz and of Shackle are radically different approaches to entrepreneurship. The neoclassical approach (represented by Schultz) in effect brings us back to a world of full equilibrium, a world in which the volume and the value of entrepreneurial activity are responses to and are determined by the given underlying cost and utility functions. The alternative approach (which I have associated with Shackle) in effect deploys the originative aspects of entrepreneurship to rebel vigorously against the relevance of any theoretical construction, such as equilibrium theory, that sees market phenomena as determinate, inexorable market responses to the preferences and constraints characterizing the given situation. The neoclassical view implies exclusion of all true novelty and surprise from our explanations; the alternative view points to the exclusion of explanations other than those that run in terms of the novelty, spontaneity, and intrinsic unpredictability of human choices. The view expressed in this book is at sharp variance with *both* of these extreme views concerning entrepreneurship.

The sections that follow seek to show how the "alertness" view of entrepreneurship mentioned earlier in this chapter enables us to adopt a middle course, avoiding the extreme features of each of the approaches I have outlined above.[9]

Entrepreneurial Alertness and the Best of Both Worlds

The approaches outlined in the preceding section offered us clear-cut and, indeed, seemingly inescapable options. Either we abstract from "originative" entrepreneurial activities or we discard our claims to render the world intelligible by reference to equilibrium configurations of maximizing decisions. Either we ignore the entrepreneur or we jettison the received theory of price. (It will be observed that a sense of these stark options underlay the rationalization provided earlier for the failure of microeconomists after 1920 to discuss the entrepreneur and his role.) My position in this book is that this statement of the choice facing the economic theorist is quite misleading. I claim, indeed, that the "alertness" view of entrepreneurship enables us to have the best of both worlds: we *can* incorporate entrepreneurship into the analysis without surrendering the heart of microeconomic theory. But even this statement of my position does not quite do it justice. I claim, more accurately, that *only* by incorporating entrepreneurship into microeconomic theory can the core of that theory be salvaged.

My "alertness" view of the entrepreneurial role rejects the thesis that if we attribute genuine novelty to the entrepreneur, we must necessarily treat entrepreneurially generated market events as not related to earlier market events in any systematic way. The genuine novelty I attribute to the entrepreneur consists in his spontaneous *discovery* of the opportunities marked out by earlier market conditions (or by future market conditions as they would be in the absence of his own actions). It is the opportunity for pure profit that those market conditions made possible that switches on the alertness of potential entrepreneurs, generating entrepreneurial discovery.

My view of the role of entrepreneurial discovery rejects, further, the thesis that recognition of entrepreneurial activities obscures the relevance of equilibrium configurations or that such relevance can be preserved only by compressing entrepreneurial activities, too, into the equilibrium mold. I hold, on the contrary, that entrepreneurial discoveries are the steps through which any possible tendency toward market equilibrium must proceed. So, far from being confusing "noise" masking the more enduring equilibrium relationships (reflecting underlying data), entrepreneurial activities make up, in my view, the process of mutual discovery by which alone we can imagine equilibrium ever to be approached.[10]

Another way of stating the position that underlies the remaining chapters of this book is as follows. I must reject the view that requires us to hold *either* that agents already possess relevant items of knowledge (with this option including, as a special case, possession by agents not of the relevant items of knowledge themselves, but rather, and altogether equivalently, their possession of knowledge of how to search for and obtain those relevant items of knowledge) *or* not only that agents are grossly ignorant at any given time, but also that they must, except as a matter of sheerest luck, necessarily continue to remain ignorant of the relevant items of knowledge. I maintain, rather, that human alertness at all times furnishes agents with the propensity to discover information that will be useful to them. Without resorting to any assumption of systematic, deliberate search, and without our relying on sheer luck, I postulate a continuous discovery process—an entrepreneurial discovery process—that, in the absence of external changes in underlying conditions, fuels a tendency toward equilibrium.

My position certainly does not admit a theory of price that is based upon the offensive assumption that market participants, at all times, have within their grasp full knowledge concerning relevant market data (including the decisions of other participants). Such an assumption is, in effect, embedded in the neoclassical position that sees entrepreneurship as a perceived ability to correct the allocation of misapplied resources. For processes of corrective reallocation so conceived, no genuine discovery is required at all. Such processes involve merely the systematic and inevitable following through of all the implications of knowledge already possessed at the very first moment. For me, to conceive of market processes in this way is indeed to attempt to understand markets with *no* role assigned to the creative entrepreneur.

But on the other hand, I also refuse to fall into the seductive trap offered by the opposite extreme. That extreme is to assume that because the knowledge possessed by market participants at any given moment is certainly likely to be supremely inadequate for the achievement of any kind of social optimum, we must see that ignorance as—except as a matter of sheer luck—an indelible feature of the situation. To adopt this extreme is to give up any notion of systematic market processes for which equilibrative tendencies might be relevant.

My view, therefore, sees initial market ignorance indeed as an inescapable feature of the human condition in a world of change, but also as subject to continual erosion as a result not of sheer luck, but of profit-inspired spurts of entrepreneurial discovery. Precisely because market decisions at a given time are based in large part on mutual ignorance (as well as on ignorance of physically available opportunities), the configuration of market prices is likely to offer pure profit opportunities for those able to discover where existing decisions were in fact mistaken. Here lies the source for any equilibrating tendencies that markets display.

The Economics of Entrepreneurship and the Scope of Economics

Much of what I have argued in this chapter, and will argue in subsequent chapters, can be stated in the form of a comment on the scope of economic science. At least since Robbins's *Nature and Significance of Economic Science* (1932), the scope of economics has been perceived, in mainstream economics, to coincide with that aspect of human affairs that can be described in terms of optimizing decision making. From this perspective, economic theory tended to be confined to the study of phenomena that are consistent with the assumption that all market participants simultaneously achieve relevantly constrained optimal positions. Consistent with this restriction of the scope of the discipline, attempts to account for dynamic processes have tended to take the form of what Professor Littlechild has aptly dubbed "clockwork" models, with the entire course of market events inexorably governed by the patterns of data fed into the model at the moment of its initiation.

The argument in this chapter, and in the book generally, calls in effect for widening the scope of economic analysis. I argue that, if the major teachings of received microeconomic theory are to be sustained, we must quite explicitly transcend the boundaries of merely optimizing decisionmaking. To understand the systematic forces at work in markets, we must introduce into our analysis the element of undeliberate but motivated *discovery*. At the level of individual market participants in general, I have elsewhere argued that this calls for extending the scope of analysis to embrace what Ludwig von Mises called *human action*. At the level of the analysis of market roles, this calls for incorporating analysis of the effect of the *entrepreneurial role*, not as a disturbing feature muddying the clear-cut outcomes mapped by economic theory, but as the essential driving force rendering that theory intelligible. The chapters that follow represent attempts to understand the systematic character of the capitalist process in terms of entrepreneurial discovery.

TWO

The Primacy of Entrepreneurial Discovery

Introduction

An economically successful society is one whose members pursue the "right" set of coordinated actions. The "ideal" economic organization for a society consists, therefore, of the pattern of institutions and incentives that will promote the pursuit of the "correct" set of actions by its members. Economic theory has, in general terms, been able to enunciate the conditions to be fulfilled if a set of actions is to be "correct." These optimality conditions are, not surprisingly, governed basically by the available resources and technological possibilities, on the one hand, and, on the other, by the pattern of consumers' tastes. The "economic problem" faced by society is then often viewed as being somehow to ensure that the various economic agents in society indeed undertake those actions that will, all together, satisfy the conditions for optimality. While this formulation is in some respects not quite satisfactory, it will serve reasonably well in introducing my discussion of the role of entrepreneurial discovery.

Patterns of Economic Organization

In theory there exist a variety of possible patterns of economic organization for society, ranging from completely centralized decision making at one extreme,

Reprinted with permission from Israel M. Kirzner et al., *The Prime Mover of Progress: The Entrepreneur in Capitalism and Socialism*, ed. A. Seldon (London: Institute of Economic Affairs, 1980).

through an array of "mixed" systems, to pure laissez-faire. Several related observations may be made.

First, *all* these possible systems of economic organization involve making *decisions*—with greater or lesser degree of decentralization.

Second, these decisions will necessarily involve an *entrepreneurial element*—regardless of the degree of decentralization sought.

Third, one dimension along which the effectiveness of each of the alternative patterns of societal economic organization will need to be assessed will therefore be that of measuring the *success with which entrepreneurial activity can be evoked in that pattern of organization.*

These observations call for some elaboration.

THE ENTREPRENEURIAL ELEMENT IN DECISIONS

I have asserted that decisions necessarily involve an entrepreneurial element. What do I mean by the "entrepreneurial element" in decision?

The *non*entrepreneurial element in decisions is easy to pin down. In most textbooks of microeconomics, this nonentrepreneurial element is often made to appear the *only* element in decision making. The nonentrepreneurial element in decision making consists of the task of calculation. A decision maker is, in this context, seen as seeking to achieve an array of goals (or to "maximize" some goal or utility function) with the scarce resources available. In seeking to arrive at the optimal decision, the decision maker must therefore calculate the solution to what, in the jargon of economics, is called a "constrained maximization problem."[1] Correct decision making, in this nonentrepreneurial sense, means correct calculation; faulty decision making is equivalent to mistakes in arithmetic.

This nonentrepreneurial aspect does not have to assume initial omniscience; it is entirely possible for the incompletely informed decision maker to calculate (i.e., to decide) how much knowledge to acquire.[2] But this non-entrepreneurial aspect does presume, at least, that the decision maker has a clear perception of the scope of his ignorance and of how this ignorance can be reduced; in a sense he knows precisely what it is that he does not know. And it is here that we can recognize the scope for the other element in decision making, the entrepreneurial element.

For the truth is that the calculative aspect is far from being the most obvious and most important element in decisions. When a wrong decision has been made, the error is unlikely to have been a mistake in calculation. It is far more likely to have resulted from an erroneous assessment of the situation—in being overoptimistic about the availability of means or about the outcomes to be expected of given actions; in pessimistically underestimating the means at one's disposal or the results to be expected from specific courses of action. Making the "right" decision, therefore, calls for far more than the correct mathematical calculation; it calls for a shrewd and wise assessment of the realities (both present and future) within the context of which the decision must be taken. It is with this aspect of decision that we will be dealing in analyzing the entrepreneurial element in subsequent discussion.

No matter how centralized or decentralized a decision-making system may be, its decision makers will regret their decisions if the entrepreneurship embodied in these decisions is of poor quality. Whatever the institutional context, a correct decision calls for reading the situation correctly; it calls for recognizing the true possibilities and for refusing to be deluded into seeing possibilities where none exist; it requires that true possibilities should not be overlooked, but that true limitations not be overlooked either. It is therefore my contention that alternative systems of economic organization have to be appraised, in part, with an eye to the respective success with which they can evoke entrepreneurship of high quality.

It is by now fairly well recognized that standard economic theory has developed along lines that virtually exclude the entrepreneurial role. This has largely been a result of the tendencies, long dominant in neoclassical economics, to exclude all elements of unexpected change, to focus attention almost exclusively on equilibrium states of affairs, and to treat individual decisions as immune from the hazards of error.[3]

As Frank Knight of Chicago explained many years ago, in a world from which the troublesome demon of unexpected change has been exorcized, it is not difficult to imagine away any need for entrepreneurship.[4] In such a world we can reasonably expect decision makers, given sufficient time, to have come somehow to perceive the world correctly. To decide, in such a world, involves nothing more than to perform those calculations we have described as constituting the nonentrepreneurial element in decision making.

In a world of unchanging certainty, where the future unfolding of events is anticipated with assurance and accuracy, selecting the optimal course of action is not a task that challenges the entrepreneurial qualities of vision, daring, and determination. Indeed, it is difficult to imagine how such a world could ever fail to be in anything but a state of optimality. To be sure, such a world must be envisaged as bounded by resource scarcities. But it is difficult to imagine how anyone in such a world—given these resource limitations, and given the accepted structure of ownership—can ascribe any perceived shortcomings to faulty decision making. Such an imaginary world is not paradise, but it can hardly fail to be the closest to paradise imaginable within the given limitations of supply and the given institutional framework.

When this theoretical framework is uncritically

adopted, it becomes easy to fall into the error of tackling economic problems with nonentrepreneurial analytical tools. It becomes natural to assume that the correct decisions are being made, from the viewpoint of the relevant decision makers; that the problems encountered are to be attributed to inadequate resources or to a faulty institutional structure. What is overlooked, in such treatments, is the possibility that a great deal of want and misery are the result of nothing less mundane than *sheer error* on the part of decision makers, that is, of decisions made that, from the decision maker's *own* point of view, are suboptimal. That such errors may and do occur requires us to recognize scope for entrepreneurial error, for decisions made with faulty assessments of the facts of the world, future as well as present, upon which the decision is to impinge.

Certainly, in a perspective which simply assumes that decision makers, in all circumstances, regardless of institutional environment, inevitably and unerringly find their way to the correct decisions there is little point in inquiring into the circumstances that are most conducive to alert, entrepreneurially successful decision making. It is a fundamental insight—upon which, I believe, the proceedings of today's colloquium are being conducted—that simply to assume correct decision making is to beg far too large a fraction of the essential question confronting us. We begin, in other words, with a healthy awareness that the world is very far from being the best of all possible worlds—even from being the best of those worlds possible with available resources and within existing institutional environments.

It is from this beginning that we are led to appreciate the primordial importance of our question: What institutional circumstances or arrangements, which system of economic and political institutions, can be expected most successfully to evoke those qualities of entrepreneurial alertness upon which the quest for optimality in decision making necessarily depends?

ENTREPRENEURSHIP AS A SCARCE RESOURCE

It might perhaps be argued that, important as the quality of entrepreneurship undoubtedly is, it does not involve any really new considerations beyond those usually taken into account in studying the conditions for optimality. All that has been established in the preceding pages, it may be held, is merely that we must bear in mind the need for a special resource, entrepreneurship, which has often been incorrectly taken for granted. Instead of viewing entrepreneurship as exercised flawlessly, tirelessly, and universally, we must begin to recognize that it is a scarce, valuable resource of which our economic models had better begin to take careful account. But all this, it may perhaps be maintained, does not justify our demand that we transcend the standard maximizing model of decision making. All that has to be done, it may be contended, is to incorporate into our list of required resources the flow of required entrepreneurial services and to ensure that available stocks of such service flows be used optimally. Social optimality, it may be contended, will now be judged within a broader framework in which there is recognition of both the demand for, and availability of, the service of entrepreneurial vision.

More particularly, in respect of the question I have described as primordial, it may be objected that it is fundamentally inappropriate to inquire into the comparative effectiveness of alternative institutional frameworks, for the evocation of entrepreneurship. It will be objected that, since entrepreneurship is a resource no different, for pure theory, from other resources, any comparison among alternative social economic systems must begin with the assumption of some *given*, initial stock of that resource. It will not do to begin a comparison between different economic systems by suggesting that the very pattern of institutional arrangement may have important implications for the initial size of a particular stock of resource. Different economic systems may certainly differ in the efficiency with which they deploy and allocate given resource supplies; but, it may be argued, if we postulate some given supply of a particular resource in one economic system, there can be no objection in principle to supposing any other system to begin with exactly the same supply of that resource.

My response to this line of argument (and thus my defense of the validity of the central question to be addressed here) rests on the insight that entrepreneurship cannot usefully be treated simply as a resource, similar in principle to the other resources available to an economic system.

The Primacy of Entrepreneurship

What is important is to insist that entrepreneurial alertness differs in fundamental respects from the resources ordinarily discussed in decision making. These differences will justify my contention that there may be important differences between different economic systems in respect to their success in harnessing entrepreneurial alertness for making error-free decisions.

A cardinal quality of a potential resource, in the economists' analysis of decisions, is that the decision maker can deploy it, if he so chooses, in specific processes geared toward the achievement of specified goals. What the decision maker has to decide is whether to deploy a particular resource, and how and in what quantity to deploy it. He must decide whether to use it at all, and whether to use it for one purpose or for another. The quality of entrepreneurial alertness cannot be discussed in these terms.

Entrepreneurial Alertness Is Not a Conventional Economic Resource. If an entrepreneur's discovery of a lucrative arbitrage opportunity galvanizes him into immediate action to capture the perceived gain, it will not do to describe the situation as one in which the entrepreneur has "decided" to use his alertness to capture this gain. He has not "deployed" his hunch for a specific purpose; *rather, his hunch has propelled him to make his entrepreneurial purchase and sale.* The entrepreneur never sees his hunches as potential inputs about which he must decide whether they are to be used. To decide *not* to use a hunch means—if it means anything at all—that a businessman realizes that he has no hunch (or that his hunch is that it will be best to be inactive for the time being). If one has become sufficiently alerted to the existence of an opportunity—that is, one has become sufficiently convinced regarding the facts of a situation—it becomes virtually impossible to imagine *not* taking advantage of the opportunity so discovered.

Entrepreneurship is thus not something to be deliberately introduced into a potential production process: it is, instead, something primordial to the very idea of a potential production process awaiting possible implementation. Entrepreneurial alertness is not an ingredient *to be deployed* in decision making; it is rather something in which *the decision itself is embedded* and without which it would be unthinkable.

It is true that *knowledge* (e.g., in the sense of technical expertise) may be deployed. A person may certainly decide that it does not pay to use his knowledge in a specific manner. Or he may decide that it does pay to use it. Here knowledge is a resource at the disposal of the entrepreneur. He is conscious of his knowledge as something to be used or not. But this refers only to knowledge of how to achieve specific goals, not knowledge of whether it is worthwhile to attempt to achieve a goal at all. A distinguishing feature of entrepreneurial insight consists precisely in the absence of awareness by its possessor that he does possess it. A would-be entrepreneur may agonize over whether to embark on a particular venture. His trauma arises not from deciding whether to use his entrepreneurial vision; it stems from his unsureness of what he "sees."

Entrepreneurial Opportunity May Be Blocked by Lack of a Resource but Not of Insight. Again, it is integral to a necessary resource (in the usual sense) that a decision maker may feel its lack. A decision maker may say, "I have all the ingredients necessary to produce ice cream, except sugar." The opportunity to achieve a particular goal is blocked only by lack of some necessary resource. But it is absurd to imagine a decision maker saying (on a commercial venture about the profitability of which he is profoundly skeptical) that he sees a profitable opportunity the exploitation of which is blocked only by lack of entrepreneurial insight. It would be absurd because this entrepreneur is (correctly or otherwise) convinced that he does *not* see any profitable opportunity in this venture at all.

To repeat what was stated earlier, all this does not apply to *technical* knowledge which an entrepreneur may know exists and which he knows he lacks. It is certainly possible for a decision maker to say, "I have all the ingredients for ice cream, but I lack the relevant recipe." He may know that a recipe exists, and that it is a good one, without knowing what it is. But for a man to refrain from a particular productive venture because he is not convinced that it is sound—even if it turns out that he was wrong—is not to refrain from it because he has been unable to lay hands on the appropriate vision; it is to refrain because he is convinced (rightly or wrongly) that, with respect to this venture, the *best entrepreneurial alertness finds nothing to be seen.*

Entrepreneurial Alertness Is Not a Potential Stock Available to Society. It is because of this inherent *primacy* of entrepreneurial alertness and vision (as contrasted with deployable resources)[5] that we cannot avoid the question to be addressed in this paper—the varying degrees of success with which alternative economic systems can inspire entrepreneurial alertness. We do not view the *potential* stock of entrepreneurial alertness in a society as some quantity "available to be used by society." (Were this the case one could proceed to inquire how different systems variously succeed in most effectively using this uniformly *given* stock.) Instead we recognize the quality of entrepreneurial alertness as something which *somehow emerges into view at the precise moment when decisions have to be made.* As we shall see, this opens up the important possibility that the institutional framework within which decisions are made may itself vitally affect the alertness out of which those decisions emerge.

The Cost of Entrepreneurship

This line of argument points to a further related insight: *entrepreneurship is costless.* In using any quantity of a scarce resource (in the usual sense of that term) the decision maker is always viewed as choosing between alternative goals to which the scarce resource might be applied. The goal forgone is the cost of using the resource for its present purpose. In the case of entrepreneurial alertness, however, a decision maker never considers whether to apply some given potential alertness to the discovery of opportunity A or opportunity B. As already argued, the opportunities (or any one of them) are either perceived or not perceived; alertness is not something about which a decision can be made *not* to deploy it. (In this we distinguish sharply between pure alertness, on the one hand, and "deployable" scarce inputs that may be useful in decision making, for example, time, technical knowledge, managerial expertise, on the other.) To recognize that opportunity A exists need not preclude simultaneously recognizing that opportunity B exists.

Conversely, to fail to recognize that opportunity A exists cannot be explained in terms of the high cost of so recognizing it; if opportunity A has not been recognized, the failure represents some shortcoming in entrepreneurial alertness, not the outcome of a decision to deploy it for the discovery of other opportunities.

Faulty Entrepreneurship Means Alertness Remains Untapped. That in the real world we encounter innumerable instances of faulty and inadequate entrepreneurship must be interpreted, therefore, not as evidence of the absolute scarcity of entrepreneurial alertness (with the existing stock of it having been applied elsewhere), but as evidence that the alertness costlessly available has somehow remained latent and untapped. The central question then looms even more significantly than ever: What institutional frameworks are best suited to tap the reservoir of entrepreneurial alertness which is certainly present—in potentially inexhaustible supply—among the members of society?

The Qualities of Entrepreneurship—the Uncharted Frontier

Although, as Ludwig von Mises pointed out long ago,[6] *all* individual action is entrepreneurial, and although I have described entrepreneurial alertness as in principle inexhaustible, I have also been careful to notice that potential alertness may be (and so often is) untapped and inert. We know, certainly, that individuals display vastly different degrees of entrepreneurial alertness. Some are quick to spot as yet unnoticed opportunities, others notice only the opportunities revealed by the discoveries of others. In some societies, in some climates, among some groups, it appears that entrepreneurial alertness is keener than in others. Studies of economic development have come to recognize that the qualities called for in successful entrepreneurship are not uniformly distributed and certainly do not appear to be in infinite supply.

It would certainly be desirable to be able to identify with precision those human qualities, personal and psychological, which are to be credited with successful entrepreneurial alertness, drive, and initiative. It would be most valuable to be able to study the short-run and long-run impact upon the development of these "entrepreneurial" qualities of alternative social, economic, and institutional frameworks. It would be important to know, for example, if a comfortable sense of security discourages noticing new opportunities. If "independence" or "economic freedom" encourages entrepreneurial drive and initiative, this would be significant information. Likewise, does "competition" encourage alertness to new opportunities?

Research on Psychological Aspects Is Desirable. Up to the present, little systematic work appears to have been done on these questions. Observations made are likely to be based on "common sense" or on anecdotal foundations. It is certainly necessary to go beyond this elementary stage. Indeed, an important frontier of knowledge, largely unexplored, appears to consist of those aspects of psychology, such as temperament, thirst for adventure, ambition, and imagination, that are likely to throw light on the development of the qualities of entrepreneurship and on the ways alternative institutional arrangements may affect such development. It is to be expected and very much to be desired that research should proceed on this frontier during the years ahead.

Applied entrepreneurial theorists should look to this research with considerable interest; it is to be hoped that their own needs and interests will help to define the directions along which this research proceeds and to formulate the questions it seeks to answer.

My tentative observations here will suggest that a number of important general statements can be made even before we enjoy the systematic knowledge I anticipate will emerge from research into the psychology of entrepreneurship.

The Incentive for Entrepreneurial Discovery

Were entrepreneurship a scarce resource in the usual sense, economists would have no difficulty in spelling out, at least in general terms, the kinds of incentives capable of coaxing out the desired quantity of entrepreneurial discovery. Potential entrepreneurs would have to be offered rewards that more than offset the costs of exercising entrepreneurship. This, after all, is how economists understand the role of incentives; this is how the price system is perceived to offer, via the resource market, the incentives required to stimulate resource supply and to allocate it among alternative uses. But the special aspects of entrepreneurship render this kind of incentive system inappropriate to entrepreneurial alertness and discovery.

Since entrepreneurship is costless (no incentive at all is needed, in principle, to activate entrepreneurial vision), and since on the other hand entrepreneurial vision is not uniformly and continuously "switched on" to take advantage of all opportunities, we are very much concerned to identify what it is that *does* "switch on" entrepreneurial vision and discovery.

With scarce resources in the usual sense, it is meaningful to talk of the kind of incentive that needs to be "offered" to owners to stimulate supply. We can imagine, that is, that some entrepreneur already has a fairly clear picture of the results to be obtained from deploying the relevant resource in some particular line of production. We can then talk of whether it is worthwhile for him to offer the resource price required to overcome the cost of supplying the resource. The point is that the notion of a needed incentive, in this usual sense, presupposes the clear perception, even before the deployment of the service, of its usefulness in production.

As has already been emphasized, such a perception is ruled out by definition in the case of entrepreneurial alertness. No one "hires" or "offers incentives" to the entrepreneur. To hire an "entrepreneur" *is to be an entrepreneur*—simply shifting the problem back to the incentives that might galvanize *this* latter entrepreneur into action. It cannot be sufficiently emphasized that (a) until an opportunity *has* been discovered, no one knows how much to offer as an incentive for its discovery; and (*b*) once the opportunity has been discovered, it is no longer relevant to inquire into the springs of entrepreneurship—since it will already have been exercised.

The Promise of Pure Gain Is Entrepreneurial Incentive. There seems one statement, however, that can be made about the incentives required to excite entrepreneurial alertness. It is a statement which sees such incentives as having little in common with the character of and role for incentives in the usual sense. It can be stated with considerable confidence *that human beings tend to notice that which it is in their interest to notice.* Human beings notice "opportunities" rather than "situations." They notice, that is, concatenations of events, realized or prospective, which offer *pure gain*. It is not the abstract *concatenation* of these events which evokes notice; it is the circumstance that these events offer the promise of pure *gain*—broadly understood to include fame, power, prestige, even the opportunity to serve a cause or to help other individuals.

Two individuals walk through the same city block teeming with hundreds of people in a variety of garbs, with shops of different kinds, advertising signs for many goods, buildings of different architectural styles. Each of these individuals will notice a different set of items out of these countless impressions impinging on his senses. What is noticed by the one is not what is noticed by the other. The difference will not merely be one of chance. It is a difference that can be ascribed, in part, to the *interests* of the two individuals. Each tends to notice what is of interest *to him*.

A difference between the price of apples traded in one part of the market and the price of apples traded in another part may pass unnoticed. It is less likely to pass unnoticed if it constitutes a phenomenon of interest to its potential discoverer. A concatenation of possible events (in this case the possible purchase of apples at a lower price, to be followed by their sale at a higher price) may not be noticed at all unless the potential discoverer stands to gain from the price differential. *In order to "switch on" the alertness of a potential discoverer to socially significant opportunities, they must offer gain to the potential discoverer himself.*

This kind of incentive—the incentive that somehow converts a socially desirable opportunity into a personally gainful one—is not needed to ensure pursuit of that opportunity *after* its discovery. Once the socially desirable opportunity has been perceived, individuals may be persuaded (or threatened) to act on that opportunity simply by suitable choice of reward (or punishment). The kind of incentive here under discussion is that required to reveal opportunities that have *until now been perceived by no one at all.*

Performance of Alternative Economic Systems under Entrepreneurial Incentive

How do alternative socioeconomic systems appear likely to perform in terms of this kind of incentive? We will consider a free market economy, a centralized (socialist) economic system, and a regulated market economy. Our concern is solely with the comparative scope they hold for entrepreneurial incentives.

ENTREPRENEURSHIP IN THE FREE MARKET

The free market is characterized most distinctively, for our purpose, *by freedom of entrepreneurial entry.* Given some accepted system of property rights, individual participants are free to enter into mutually beneficial trades with each other. Production decisions involve judgments about buying inputs on factor markets in order to sell output in product markets. Market prices therefore guide the decisions which determine the allocation of society's resources among alternative lines of output. Were the market to have attained full equilibrium, it may, under specific assumptions, be described as having attained an optimal allocation of resources.[7] But (especially in view of ambiguities surrounding the interpretation of "social optimum" and of the possibility that not all the specific assumptions will be fulfilled in practice) this is *not* the interesting proposition—even were it reasonable to view the free market economy as in continuous equilibrium.

What is important about the market economy is that unexploited opportunities for reallocating resources from one (low market valued) use to another of higher value offer the opportunity for pure entrepreneurial gain. A misallocation of resources occurs because, so far, market participants have not noticed the price discrepancy involved. This price discrepancy presents itself as an opportunity to be exploited by its discoverer. *The most impressive aspect of the market system is the tendency for such opportunities to be discovered.*

The Discovery Process of the Market. It is in a sense similar to this that Hayek has referred to the competitive market process as a "discovery procedure".[8] The essence is not that market prices offer spontaneously developed "signals" able faultlessly to coordinate millions of independently made decisions. (This would occur only in equilibrium; in disequilibrium the prices which prevail would *not* so perfectly coordinate decisions.) It is rather that the disequilibrium situation—in which prices do not offer the correct signals—is one which offers entrepreneurs the incentives required for the discrepancies to be noticed and corrected. In the course of this entrepreneurial process, new products may be introduced, new qualities of existing products may be developed, new methods of production may be ventured, new forms of industrial organization, financing, marketing, or tackling risk may be developed. All the ceaseless churning and agitation of the market is to be understood as the conse-

quence of the never-ending discovery process of which
the market consists.

ENTREPRENEURSHIP IN THE SOCIALIZED ECONOMY

Little work has been done on the analysis of entrepreneurship in fully socialized societies. The great
debate on economic calculation under socialism carried
on between the two world wars in many respects revolved
around precisely this issue but was couched in terms
which unfortunately permitted its central importance to
be overlooked. The attempts by Oskar Lange (of Poland)
and others to show how a socialist system could be set up
that would permit decentralized decisions by managers of
socialist enterprises on the basis of centrally promulgated
"prices," along the same lines as the price system under
the free market, unfortunately completely overlooked the
entrepreneurial character of the price system.

Lange relied on the "parametric function" of prices,
that is, on that aspect of prices which permits each decision maker to treat them as equilibrium prices to which
he must passively adjust himself.[9] But in this view of the
market (and hence of the possibility of a socialist "price"
system), Lange failed to recognize that the distinctive aspect of the market is the manner in which prices *change*,
that is, that market prices are in fact treated nonpara-
metrically. It is one thing to imagine that socialist managers can be motivated to obey rules on the basis of
centrally promulgated "prices"; it is quite another to take
it for granted that the *non*parametric function of price (in
which, that is, price is *not* being treated as a datum but is
subject to change by individual market participants), a
function which depends entirely on entrepreneurial discovery of *new* opportunities for pure profit, can be simulated in a system from which the private entrepreneurial
function is completely absent.

Alertness by "Price" Planners and Plant Managers. Under a Lange-type system, alertness would be called for at a

number of levels. Officials deciding on the "price" structure must do so by what they know about the performance of the economy under earlier "price" structures
and by what they anticipate to be the pattern of consumer
demand and of resource supply in the period ahead. In
promulgating a list of "prices" it is necessary to determine, first of all, the list of commodities and of resource
services for which "prices" are to be set. The construction of this list requires an enormous volume of entrepreneurial alertness on the part of these officials. After
all, some products should not be produced at all; others
very definitely ought to be produced, but officials may be
quite ignorant of them or of their urgency. This is of
course more particularly likely to be true of new and innovative products and product qualities. But it could occur with any product whatever.

Again, the Lange system would call for alertness by
socialist plant managers. They would have to identify
sources of resource supply; they would have to notice
technological possibilities that may not hitherto have
been known, or that, given the old price structure, may
not have been economic. They would have to notice the
need for and possibility of any number of changes (innovative or otherwise) which changed patterns of tastes, for
example, might make worthwhile. There is certainly
nothing in Lange's own description of his system to suggest how this might be ensured.

Will Available Options Be Noticed? How? The question
the entrepreneurial theorist must ask is not whether,
given available known options, the relevant socialist official is operating under an incentive system that will
make it personally gainful for him to select the optimal
course of action for society. Our question is rather whether there is any assurance that relevant options will in
practice be noticed as being available. What might motivate an official to notice an opportunity not yet adopted
(but which it might be highly valuable to pursue)? It will

not do to suggest that some higher official arrange matters so that when the (lower) official does notice the opportunity he can personally benefit by its adoption. This merely passes our question up the line: What might motivate this higher official to notice the opportunity?—and even to notice its worthwhileness *after* it has been brought to his attention?

We will, for the present, ignore the question of how a newly discovered valuable social opportunity is revealed, even after the event, as having been such. Our question will confine itself to asking how it might be ensured that such social opportunities constitute at the same time privately gainful opportunities for their potential discoverers. It is doubful in the extreme if ideals such as benevolence or patriotism can be relied upon, in general, to enable a potential discoverer to identify his own personal interest with that of the discovery of an opportunity for a reallocation of resources desirable for society.

We might imagine, of course, a system in which there is not merely decentralization of decision making, in the Lange sense, but also freedom for socialist managers to buy and sell on behalf of the state (when discrepancies among socialist "prices" might have been discovered) and to retain for themselves some fraction of the price differential. If such trading is restricted to those who are already socialist managers, we will have to examine the mechanism of selection of managers to see whether it indeed ensures that those with entrepreneurial skills tend to become socialist managers (since the socialist state would not be permitting others to "prove" their entrepreneurial skills in this way). On the other hand, if entrepreneurial trading is to be open for all (raising, let me of course note, the obvious question of access to society's capital to be risked in such ventures), then clearly we have moved closer and closer toward a "mixed" capitalist system in which private entrepreneurs might be free to seek profits within a system of state-controlled prices (a regulated system which will be briefly considered below).

Individual Decision Makers Cannot Profit under "Market" Socialist Schemes. We may talk of various schemes for "market" socialism along Lange's lines, in which some decisions are left to lower-ranking officials to be made on the basis of centrally designed systems of "prices." No matter how extensive the degree of decentralization thus achieved, however, a critical condition for the socialist quality of the system appears to be that neither at the level of the central design of "prices," nor of individual managers' decisions made on the basis of these "prices" may decisions be made primarily in order that the decision maker can profit personally from errors discovered. Those responsible for designing the system of socialist "prices" are clearly not participants in any entrepreneurial market; their function is to impose "prices" upon the socialist "market."

To imagine that in this socialist "market" freedom of entry for private profit-making entrepreneurial activity is to be permitted is surely to compromise fatally the definition of a socialist economic system. But without such freedom of entrepreneurial entry, market socialism has a fatal flaw: it has not succeeded in identifying any way by which errors, whether of omission or commission, can be systematically avoided by decision makers. It has not identified any way the discovery and avoidance of error redounds directly to the personal benefit of the discoverer. It has not identified how the unsuspectedly inefficient socialist venture might so reveal itself to a socialist decision maker in advance as a threat to his own wellbeing; it has not identified how the currently undreamed of venture, of critical benefit to society, might reveal itself to a socialist planner as one offering him personal gain.

Incentives to Socialist Managers Deny the Essential Role of Entrepreneurial Discovery. I do not deny the possibility of arranging incentives to socialist managers to produce more, or to produce with a smaller labor force or lower energy consumption. Nor do I even deny the possibility of offering incentives that will reward innovation. Incentives can certainly be structured to reward inventors and innovators of new products and new production techniques. Recent extensive study of innovation in the Soviet Union has, for example, confirmed the significant vitality of the innovative process there (although the process lags more or less behind that in capitalist economies).[10] But to reward managers for meeting or exceeding target output quantities presupposes that *it is already known* that more of these outputs is urgently required by society; to reward managers for introducing a new product is to presume that *it is already known* that this particular new product—or else *any* new product—is socially more important (taking into account the resources required for its production) than the product it replaces; to reward managers for introducing innovative methods of production is to presume that *it is already known* that the additional inputs called for by the new technique are less costly to society than those the technique avoids—or else that *any* change in production technique must be an improvement over those currently employed.

That these matters may already be known is in many instances entirely plausible. But if they *are* assumed already known, we are simply assuming away the need for entrepreneurial discovery. The task is to ensure the discovery—by someone, somewhere, who possesses power to set things into motion—of which products (existing or new) should be produced (and in what quantities), the urgency of which the current conventional wisdom has *failed* to recognize. The problem is to identify techniques of production whose usefulness has up until now *not* been perceived. Not all innovation is socially desirable; not all expansion of lines of output is socially desirable. What is required is an incentive system to convince decision makers that when they discover opportunities others will deny to exist, they (the discoverers) will be the gainers.

Thus, far, in all the discussion of varieties of socialism, of incentive systems and planning theories, I have not seen *this* problem addressed. Nor is it at all apparent how, without fundamentally compromising the essential defining criteria for socialism, it can be solved.

ENTREPRENEURSHIP IN THE REGULATED MARKET ECONOMY[11]

Most societies in the modern world have allowed their economic systems to follow neither the pattern of pure socialism nor that of pure capitalism. They consist of market economies that have been circumscribed by more or less extensive systems of state intervention. Convinced that the unhampered market will generate undesirable price structures or undesirable arrays of output qualities, working conditions, or other undesirables, the state intervened, replacing the laissez-faire market by the regulated market. Price ceilings and price and wage floors, transfer of income, imposed safety standards, child labor laws, zoning laws, prohibited industrial integration, prohibited competition, imposed health warnings, compulsory old-age pensions, and prohibited drugs are among the countless controls that possibly well-meaning public officials impose. What is the role of entrepreneurial discovery in the regulated market?

Genuine—but Inhibited—Entrepreneurial Incentive. Despite the controls, regulations, and interventions, there exist in such systems genuine markets for both resource services and consumer products. Although the prices which emerge in regulated markets may have been more or less drastically distorted in the regulatory process, they are (except for directly controlled prices) nonetheless market prices. To the extent that entrepreneurial entry remains free, discrepancies in these prices provide the incentives for entrepreneurs to capture pure profit, leading to a process of entrepreneurial competition acting at all times to modify the existing price structure.

Nevertheless, it is not difficult to perceive the many ways entrepreneurial discovery may come to be inhibited or redirected under regulatory constraints. And regulation raises new and important questions concerning the way the agents of the state (whether legislators or officials in other stages of regulation and its enforcement) come to notice where opportunities for supposedly beneficial regulation may exist. Let us take up these latter questions first.

Knowledge and Discovery Are Absent in Price Setting and Resource Allocation. Government regulation takes the general form of imposed price floors, price ceilings, mandated quality specifications, and similar measures. We will assume that the hope surrounding such government impositions is that they will confine market activities to desired channels and at desired levels. But it is by no means clear how officials will know what prices to set, or if their earlier decisions have been in error. It is not clear how officials will *discover* those opportunities for improving the allocation of resources (which, after all, we can hardly assume to be automatically known at the outset of a regulatory endeavor). The regulator's estimates of the prices consumers are prepared to pay, or of the prices resource owners are prepared to accept, are not *profit-motivated* estimates. But estimates of market demand conditions, or of market supply conditions, that are not profit motivated cannot reflect the powerful, discovery-inspiring incentives of the entrepreneurial quest for profit.

It is, further, not clear how it can be ensured that government officials who perceive market conditions more accurately than others will tend systematically to replace less competent regulators. It is not clear what proxy for entrepreneurial profit and loss there might be that could inspire officials to see personal gain for themselves in successful discovery. What regulators know (or believe they know) at a given moment is presumably only partly correct. No systematic process seems available through which regulators might come to discover what they have not known, especially since they have not known that they enjoy less than complete awareness of relevant situations. *If they do not know what they do not know, how will they know what remains to be discovered?*

Quite apart from the question of the entrepreneurship required to engage in regulation believed to be desirable, we must, in the context of the regulated market economy, also consider the impact of regulation upon the pattern and direction of entrepreneurial discovery in the marketplace. There is a serious likelihood that regulatory constraints may bar the discovery of pure profit opportunities (and thus of possibilities for socially beneficial resource reallocation).

Damaging Effects of Regulatory Controls and Price Ceilings. A good deal of regulation consists in creating *barriers to entry.* Tariffs, licensing requirements, labor legislation, airline regulation, and bank regulation, for example, do not merely limit numbers in particular markets. These kinds of regulatory activity tend to bar entry to entrepreneurs who believe they have discovered profit opportunities in barred areas of the market. Such barriers may, by removing the personal gain which entrepreneurs might have reaped by their discoveries, bring it about that *some opportunities may simply not be discovered by anyone.* An entrepreneur who knows that he will not be able to enter the banking business may simply not notice opportunities in the banking field that might otherwise have seemed obvious to him; those who are already in banking, and who have failed to see these opportunities, may continue to overlook them. Protection from entrepreneurial competition does not provide any spur to entrepreneurial discovery.

Imposed price ceilings may, similarly, not merely generate discoordination in the markets for existing goods and services (as is of course well recognized in the theory of price controls); they may inhibit the discovery of wholly new opportunities. A price ceiling does not merely block the upper reaches of a given supply curve—further increases in supply to meet demand. It may also inhibit the discovery of as yet unsuspected sources of supply (which in the absence of the ceiling might have shifted the entire supply curve to the right—made supplies marketable at lower prices—as these sources came to be discovered) or of wholly unknown new products.

The imposition of price ceilings, which has switched off the lure of pure profits in this way, is not accompanied, as far as can be seen, by any device that might, in some alternative manner, lead a potential discoverer to associate a discovery with his own personal gain.

Conclusion

This discussion has focused attention on a neglected aspect of economic decision making, the urgency for incentives for the "entrepreneurial" discovery of what opportunities exist for economic action. Pursuing this point further, I have pointed to the need for critical assessment, within any economic system of organization, of the way the system permits the potential discoverers to identify their own personal interest with the successful discovery of socially desirable opportunities for change. In the briefest possible framework, I have considered aspects of the socialist system and of the regulated market economy, in contrast to the laissez-faire market system.

A great deal of work is waiting to be done in the economics of entrepreneurship. It has been my purpose to emphasize the enormous stake society—under whatever economic system it may operate—holds in the successful pursuit of such research.

THREE

Uncertainty, Discovery, and Human Action: A Study of the Entrepreneurial Profile in the Misesian System

A central element in the economics of Ludwig von Mises is the role played by the entrepreneur and the function fulfilled by entrepreneurship in the market process. The character of that process for Mises is decisively shaped by the leadership, the initiative, and the driving activity displayed and exercised by the entrepreneur. Moreover, in an intellectual edifice built systematically on the notion of individual *human action*—on the manner in which reasoning human beings interact while seeking to achieve their individual purposes—it is highly significant that Mises found it of relevance to emphasize that each human actor is always, in significant respects, an entrepreneur.[1] The present paper seeks to explore the character of Misesian entrepreneurship, with special reference to the influence exercised by the inescapable uncertainty that pervades economic life. Both at the level of isolated individual human action and at the level of entrepreneurial activity in market context, I shall be con-

Reprinted by permission of the publisher from *Method, Process, and Austrian Economics: Essays in Honor of Ludwig von Mises,* edited by Israel M. Kirzner (Lexington, Mass.: Lexington Books, D. C. Heath and Company, copyright 1982, D. C. Heath and Company).

cerned to determine the extent to which the Misesian entrepreneur owes his very existence and his function to the unpredictability of his environment and to the ceaseless tides of change that undergird that unpredictability.

On the face of it, this question may not seem worthy of new research. Mises, it may be pointed out, expressed himself quite clearly on numerous occasions to the effect that the entrepreneurial function is inseparable from speculation with respect to an uncertain future. For example he wrote that "the entrepreneur is always a speculator."[2] Or again, he wrote that "entrepreneur means acting man in regard to the changes occurring in the data of the market."[3] Moreover, when Mises points out that every individual acting man is an entrepreneur, this is because "every action is embedded in the flux of time and thus involves a speculation."[4] In other words, the entrepreneurial element cannot be abstracted from the notion of individual human action, because the "uncertainty of the future is already implied in the very notion of action. That man acts and that the future is uncertain are by no means two independent matters, they are only two different modes of establishing one thing."[5]

Thus it might seem that the essentiality of uncertainty for the Misesian entrepreneur hardly needs to be established anew. Certainly any thought of questioning that essentiality must, it might appear, be quickly dismissed.

What I shall argue in this chapter is not that the role of uncertainty in the function of the Misesian entrepreneur may be any less definitive than these clear-cut statements imply, but that this role is a more subtle one than may on the surface appear to be the case. It is this subtlety in the role played by uncertainty in the Misesian system, I believe, that sets that system apart in significant respects from the views of other economists (such as Knight or Shackle) who have emphasized the phenomenon of uncertainty in the context of the market.

The Background of the Present Exploration

In earlier forays into the field of the Misesian entrepreneur, I developed an interpretation of the entrepreneurial function in which the role of uncertainty, while
recognized and certainly not denied, was not emphasized.
This failure to emphasize uncertainty was quite deliberate and was indeed explicitly acknowledged.[6] Instead of
emphasizing the uncertainty in which entrepreneurial activity is embedded, these earlier treatments stressed the
element of *alertness to hitherto unperceived opportunities* that is, I argued, crucial for the Misesian concept
of entrepreneurship.[7] Since my position explicitly recognized the element of change and uncertainty while it
claimed to be able to explicate the elusive quality of entrepreneurship without need to emphasize the uncertainty element, it is perhaps not surprising that my treatment
has drawn fire from two different perspectives. A number
of critics have felt rather strongly that failure to emphasize the role of uncertainty renders my understanding of
entrepreneurship fundamentally defective. At least one
critic, on the other hand, has been persuaded by my exposition of entrepreneurship to the point that even my
frugal references to uncertainty as an inescapable characteristic of the entrepreneurial scene appear altogether unnecessary and are seen as producing confusion. Since all
these critics are basically in agreement with me, I believe,
on the broad accuracy of the general entrepreneurial character of the market process that I ascribe to Mises, it has
for some time been my hope to delve into these questions
more thoroughly. Some further brief recapitulation of
these earlier discussions seems in order as an introduction to our present exploration.

My emphasis on alertness to hitherto unperceived
opportunities as the decisive element in the entrepreneurial function stemmed from my pursuit of a didactic
purpose. This purpose was to distinguish the analysis of
the market *process* (a process in which the entrepreneur

plays the crucial role) as sharply as possible from the analysis of equilibrium states (in which all scope for entrepreneurial activity has been assumed away). In
equilibrium, it turns out, all market decisions have somehow come already into complete mutual coordination.
Market participants have been assumed to be making
their respective decisions with perfectly correct information concerning the decisions that all other participants
are making at the same time.[8] So long as the underlying
present consumer attitudes and production possibilities
prevail, it is clear that we can rely on the very same set of
decisions being made in each of an indefinite number of
future periods. On the other hand, in the absence of such
complete equilibrium coordination of decisions, a market
process is set in motion in which market participants are
motivated to learn to anticipate more accurately the decisions of others; in this process the entrepreneurial, profit–motivated discovery of the gaps in mutual coordination of decisions is a crucial element. Entrepreneurial activity drives this market process of mutual discovery by a
continually displayed alertness to profit opportunities
(into which the market automatically translates the existing gaps in coordination). Whereas entrepreneurial activity is indeed speculative, the pursuit of profit
opportunities is a purposeful and deliberate one, the "emphasis on the element of alertness in action [was]
intended to point out that, far from being numbed by the
inescapable uncertainty of our world, men *act upon their
judgments of* what opportunities have been left unexploited by others."[9]

In developing this aspect of entrepreneurship I was
led to emphasize the capture of pure entrepreneurial profit as reducible essentially to the exploitation of arbitrage
opportunities. Imperfect mutual awareness on the part of
other market participants had generated the emergence of
more than one price for the same bundle of economic
goods; the entrepreneur's alertness to the profit opportunity presented by this price discrepancy permits him to

win these profits (and, in so doing, tends to nudge the prices into closer adjustment with each other). In so emphasizing the arbitrage character of pure profit, emphasis was deliberately withdrawn from the speculative character of entrepreneurial activity that wins pure profit by correctly anticipating *future* price movements.[10]

A number of (otherwise friendly) critics expressed serious reservations concerning my deliberate lack of stress on the speculative character of entrepreneurial activity. Henry Hazlitt pointed out that my repeated references to the entrepreneur's perceiving of opportunities fail to make clear that at best the entrepreneur *thinks* that he perceives opportunities: that what an entrepreneur "acts on may not be a perception but a *guess*."[11] Murray Rothbard has endorsed a discussion by Robert Hébert in which my definition of the entrepreneur is sharply distinguished from that of Mises: "Mises conceives of the entrepreneur as the uncertainty bearer. . . . To Kirzner, on the other hand, entrepreneurship becomes reduced to the quality of *alertness*; and uncertainty seems to have little to do with the matter."[12] Although conceding that my treatment of the entrepreneur has "a certain amount of textual justification in Mises," Rothbard sees this not as providing genuine support for my reading of the Misesian entrepreneur but as being the result of a "certain uncharacteristic lack of clarity in Mises' discussion of entrepreneurship."[13]

In a most thoughtful paper several years ago, Lawrence H. White too deplored my deliberate failure to emphasize uncertainty in the analysis of entrepreneurship. This treatment, White argues, fosters neglect of important features of entrepreneurial activity that arise precisely from the passage of time and from the uncertainty generated by the prospect of unanticipated changes bound to occur during the journey to the future. To compress entrepreneurial activity into an arbitrage box is, in particular, to fail to recognize the highly important part played by entrepreneurial *imagination*.[14]

On the other hand, my treatment of entrepreneurship has been criticized by J. High from a diametrically opposite point of view. High accepts the definition of entrepreneurship in terms of alertness to opportunities for pure profit. He proceeds to point out that "nothing in this definition requires uncertainty. The definition requires ignorance, because the opportunity has not been discovered earlier: it requires error, because the opportunity could have been discovered earlier, but the definition does not require uncertainty."[15] High is therefore critical of passages in which uncertainty is linked specifically with entrepreneurship.[16]

Clearly the role of uncertainty in the entrepreneurial environment, and in particular its relationship to the entrepreneur's alertness to error, demands further explication. What follows may not satisfy my critics (from both wings). I trust, however, that my discussion of some of the perhaps less obvious links between uncertainty and alertness will, if it does not quite absolve me of the charge of intransigence, at least bear witness to my grateful acknowledgment of the very deep importance of the problems raised by my critics.

Our inquiry will be facilitated by a careful examination of the sense in which each individual engaging in human action is, as already cited from Mises, exercising entrepreneurship.[17] Or to put the issue somewhat differently, it will be helpful to explore more precisely what it is that distinguishes human action from purely calculative, allocative, economizing activity.

I have argued in earlier work that the concept of human action emphasized by Mises includes an ineradicable entrepreneurial element that is absent from the notion of economizing, of the allocation of scarce resources among competing ends, that was articulated by Lord Robbins.[18] On the face of it there appear to be two distinct aspects of Misesian human action that might be considered to set it apart from Robbinsian economizing activity. We shall have to ask whether these are indeed two distinct aspects of human action and how they relate to the entrepreneurial element that human action contains (but which Robbinsian allocative activity does not). These two aspects of human action (not present in economizing activity) may be identified as (1) the element in action that is beyond the scope of "rationality" as an explanatory tool, and (2) the element in action that constitutes discovery of error. Let us consider these in turn.

The Limits of Rationality

Perhaps the central feature of purely economizing activity is that it enables us to explain behavior by reference to the postulate of rationality. With a given framework of ranked goals sought, and of scarce resources available to be deployed, rationality (in the narrow sense of consistency of behavior with the relevant given ranking of ends) ensures a unique pattern of resource allocation; decision making can be fully understood in the light of the given ends—means framework. There is no part of the decision that cannot be accounted for; given the framework, the decision taken is fully determined (and therefore completely explained); any other decision would have been simply unthinkable.

On the other hand, the notion of Misesian human action embraces the very adoption of the ends-means framework to be considered relevant. The adoption of any particular ends-means framework is a step which is logically (although not necessarily chronologically) prior to that of allocating means consistently with the given ranking of ends. If the human decision is to be perceived as including the selection of the ends-means framework, then we have an element in that decision that cannot, of course, be explained by reference to rationality. Consistency in action is not sufficient to account for that ranking of ends in terms of which consistency itself is to be defined. Thus the totality of human action cannot, even in principle, be explained on the basis of rationality. A science of human action cannot fail to acknowledge—

even after full recognition of the formidable explanatory power of the postulate of rationality—that human history, depending as it does on unexplained adoption of goals and awareness of means, contains a strong element of the unexplained and even the spontaneous. These are themes that have, of course, been extensively developed by G. L. S. Shackle: "Choice and reason are things different in nature and function, reason *serves* the chosen purposes, not performs the selection of them."[19] "A man can be supposed to act always in rational response to his 'circumstances': but those 'circumstances' can, *and must*, be in part the creation of his own mind. . . . In this loose-textured history, men's choices of action being choices action being choices among thoughts which spring indeterminately in their minds, we can deem them to *initiate* trains of events in some real sense."[20]

In an earlier era, much criticism of the role of the rationality postulate in economic theory focused on the place of apparently nonrational behavior, behavior arising out of impetuous impulse or out of unthinking habit.[21] It is simply unrealistic, these criticisms ran, to assume that economic activity represents the exclusive result of deliberation. Man acts all too often without careful deliberation; he does not weigh the costs and benefits of his actions. This is not the place to evaluate these criticisms or deal with the debates that they engendered three-quarters of a century ago and more. But it is perhaps important to point out that limits of rationality discussed in this section have little to do with the arguments based on impulsiveness and on habit bondage. It is not at all being argued here that human action involves the *thoughtless* selection of goals. Human decision making may of course involve the most agonizingly careful appraisal of alternative courses of action to choose what seems likely to offer the most estimable of outcomes. In emphasizing that the rationality postulate is unable to explain the selection of the relevant ends-means framework, I am not suggesting that that selection occurs without deliberation, but merely that the results of that deliberation cannot be predicted on the basis of the postulate of consistency; that deliberation is essentially creative. One may predict the answer that a competent mathematician will arrive at when he tackles a given problem in computation (in the same way that one may know in advance the answer to that problem that will be yielded by an electronic computer); but one cannot, in the same way, predict which computational problem the mathematician will deliberately choose to tackle (as one may not be able to predict which problems will be selected to be fed into the electronic computer).

The matter may be presented in an alternative version. One may always distinguish, within each human decision, an element into which thought enters in self-aware fashion from an element into which thought enters without self-awareness. A man desires a specific goal with great eagerness; but deliberation persuades him, let us imagine, that it is in his interest not to reveal that eagerness to others (say, because others might then spitefully wish to deny that goal to him). The studied nonchalance with which he masks his pursuit of the goal exhibits scope for both elements: (1) his apparent nonchalance is indeed deliberate and studied, he knows precisely the reason why it is important that he pretend lack of interest; but (2) he may not be at all self-aware as to how he arrived at this judgment to act on the assumption that others may spitefully seek to frustrate his achievement. He simply decides to act. His decision is to refrain from naively pursuing with evident eagerness what he eagerly desires; but his decision is yet naive in the sense that he has not, for example, sought (as reasons having to do with long-term strategy might well suggest) to ostentatiously pretend unawareness of the spitefulness of the others. No matter how calculative a man's behavior may be, it seems impossible to avoid having accepted, without calculation, some framework within which to self-consciously engage in cost-benefit comparisons. A man decides to display behavior a. We may call the mental activity of making that decision activity *b*. Now the man *may* have decided (in the course of decision-making activity *c*) to engage in decision-making activity *b* (or he may have simply and impulsively engaged in decision—making activity *b*). But even if engaging in decision-making activity *b* (as a result of which behavior *a* was chosen) was itself the outcome of "higher" decisions, at some level our decision maker's highest decision was made quite unselfconsciously.

This extra-Robbinsian aspect of human action, the aspect which involves the creative, unpredictable selection of the ends-means framework, can also be usefully stated in terms of *knowledge*. Given his knowledge of the relevant ends-means framework, man's decision can be predicted without doubt; it is simply a matter of computation. To the extent, however, that man must "decide" what it is, so to speak, that he knows, and that this determination is not in general based ineluctably on other knowledge unambiguously possessed, man's behavior is not at all predictable. What a man believes himself to know is not itself the result of a calculative decision.[22] This expression of the notion of the existence of limits to rationality will facilitate our insight into the important linkage that exists between these limits and the phenomenon of uncertainty.

In the absence of uncertainty it would be difficult to avoid the assumption that each individual does in fact already know the circumstances surrounding his decision. Without uncertainty, therefore, decision making would no longer call for any imaginative, creative determination of what the circumstances really are. Decision making would call merely for competent calculation. Its results could, in general, be predicted without doubt. Human judgment would have no scope. "With uncertainty absent, man's energies are devoted altogether to doing things; . . . in a world so built . . . it seems likely that . . . all organisms [would be] automata."[23] "If man knew the future, he would not have to choose and would

not act. He would be like an automaton, reacting to stim-
uli without any will of its own."[24] Thus the extra-Robbinsian aspect of human action, the aspect responsible for
rendering human action unpredictable and incompletely
explainable in terms of rationality, arises from the inherent uncertainty of human predicament. If, then, one
chooses to identify entrepreneurship with the function of
making decisions in the face of an uncertain present or
future environment, it certainly appears that Misesian
human action does (while Robbinsian economizing does
not) include an entrepreneurial element.

But before making up our minds on this point, we
must consider that second element, mentioned at the end
of the preceding section, that distinguishes Misesian
human action from Robbinsian allocative decision
making.

The Discovery of Error

To draw attention to this element in human action I
shall draw on an earlier paper in which I attempted to
identify what might represent "entrepreneurial profit" in
successful individual action in a Crusoe context.[25] Entrepreneurial profit in the Crusoe context, it turned out,
can be identified only where Crusoe discovers that he has
up until now attached an erroneously low valuation to
resources over which he has command. Until today
Crusoe has been spending his time catching fish with his
bare hands. Today he has realized that he can use his time
far more valuably by building a boat or making a net. "He
has discovered that he had placed an incorrectly low value on his time. His reallocation of his labor time from
fishing to boat-building is an entrepreneurial decision
and, assuming his decision to be a correct one, yields pure
profit in the form of additional value discovered to be
forthcoming from the labor time applied."[26] This (Crusonian) pure profit arises from the circumstance that at
the instant of entrepreneurial discovery Menger's law is

violated. Menger's law teaches that men value goods according to the value of the satisfactions that depend on possession of those goods. This law arises from man's propensity to attach the value of ends to the means needed for their achievement. At the moment of entrepreneurial discovery Crusoe realizes that the ends achievable with his labor time have higher value than the ends he had previously sought to achieve:

> The value Crusoe has until now attached to his time is *less* than the value of the ends he now seeks. This discrepancy is, at the level of the individual, pure profit. . . . Once the old ends-means framework has been completely and unquestionably replaced by the new one, of course, it is the value of the new ends that Crusoe comes to attach to his means. . . . But, during the instant of an entrepreneurial leap of faith . . . there is scope for the discovery that, indeed, the ends achieved are more valuable than had hitherto been suspected. *This*, is the discovery of pure (Crusonian) entrepreneurial profit.[27]

Scope for entrepreneurship thus appears to be grounded in the possibility of discovering error. In the market context, the state of general equilibrium, providing as it does absolutely no scope for the discovery of profitable discrepancies between prices and costs, affords no opportunity for entrepreneurial discovery and turns out to be populated entirely by Robbinsian maximizers. In the same way, it now appears, the situation in which Crusoe is errorlessly allocating his resources—with the value of ends being fully and faultlessly attached to the relevant means in strict accordance with Menger's law—affords no scope for the entrepreneurial element in human action. Human action, without scope for the discovery of error, collapses into Robbinsian allocative activity.

Clearly this way of identifying the entrepreneurial

element that is present in Misesian human action but absent in Robbinsian economizing activity fits in well with
the approach that defines entrepreneurship as alertness to
hitherto unperceived opportunities.[28] In the market context entrepreneurship is evoked by the presence of as yet
unexploited opportunities for pure profit. These opportunities are evidence of the failure of market participants,
up until now, to correctly assess the realities of the market situation. At the level of the individual too, it is then
attractive to argue, an entrepreneurial element in action
is evoked by the existence of as yet unexploited private
opportunities. To act entrepreneurially is to identify situations overlooked until now because of error.

Uncertainty and/or Discovery

Our discussion has led us to identify two apparently
distinct elements in human action, each of which possesses   plausible   claims   as   constituting   that   entrepreneurial element in action that sets it apart from
purely calculative economizing activity: (1) On the one
hand we saw that it appears plausible to associate entrepreneurship with the department within human action
in which the very framework for calculative economizing
activity is, in an open-ended, uncertain world, selected as
being relevant. It is here that we would find scope for the
unpredictable, the creative, the imaginative expressions
of the human mind—expressions that cannot themselves
be explained in terms of the postulate of consistency.
Thus entrepreneurship, at the Crusoe level, arises
uniquely and peculiarly from the circumstance that, as a
result of the inescapable uncertainty of the human predicament, acting man cannot be assumed to be sure of the
framework relevant for calculative activity. He must,
using whatever entrepreneurial gifts he can display,
choose a framework. (2) On the other hand, as we have
seen, it appears perhaps equally plausible to associate entrepreneurship with that aspect of human action in which

the alert individual realizes the existence of opportunities that he has up until now somehow failed to notice. Scope for entrepreneurship, at the Crusoe level, arises then not from the present uncertainty that must now be grappled with in decision making but from earlier error from which entrepreneurial discovery must now provide protection.

I must emphasize that these alternative identifications of the entrepreneurial element in action do appear, at least on a first scrutiny, to be genuinely different from one another. It is of course true that past error (from which, on the one view, we look to entrepreneurial discovery to provide a rescue) may be attributed to the pervasive uncertainty that characterizes our world (and to the inevitably kaleidic changes responsible for that uncertainty). But to discover hitherto unnoticed opportunities (unnoticed because of past failure to pierce correctly the fog of uncertainty) does not at all seem to be the same task as that of selecting between alternative present scenarios for the future within which calculative activity is to be undertaken. Moreover, whatever the possible reasons for past error, error itself implies merely ignorance, not necessarily uncertainty.[29] To escape ignorance is one thing; to deal with uncertainty is another.

This tension that we have discovered at the level of human action in the Crusoe context, between present uncertainty and earlier error as sources of entrepreneurship, is clearly to be linked immediately with our more general exploration in this chapter. This chapter is concerned with determining the extent to which the Misesian entrepreneur is to be perceived as the creature of uncertainty. The tension we have now discovered between present uncertainty and earlier error corresponds exactly to the disagreement we encountered between those who see the Misesian entrepreneur as essentially the bearer of market uncertainty and those who see him as the discoverer of earlier market errors. It is my contention that our awareness of this apparent tension can in fact shed light on certain subtleties in the concept of entrepreneurship likely otherwise to be overlooked. My procedure to develop this claim will be as follows: I will seek to show that, on a deeper understanding of the meaning of uncertainty and of the discovery of error at the level of individual action, the tension between them dissolves in a way that will reveal the full significance of entrepreneurial alertness at the level of the individual. Thereafter I will pursue the analogy between the scope of entrepreneurship at the individual level and that of entrepreneurship at the level of the market, drawing on this analogy to identify precisely the relative roles, in market entrepreneurship, of uncertainty and of alertness.

Action and Alertness

Man acts, in the light of the future as he envisages it, to enhance his position in that future. The realized consequences of man's actions, however, flow from the impact of those actions on the actual (as contrasted with the envisaged) course of future events. The extent to which man's plans for the enhancement of his prospects are fulfilled depends on the extent to which the future as he has envisaged it corresponds to the future as it in fact occurs. There is no natural set of forces or constraints assuring correspondence between the envisaged future and the realized future. The two may, it seems at first glance, diverge from one another with complete freedom. The future course of events is in general certainly not constrained by past forecasts; nor, unfortunately, are forecasts constrained by the actual future events these forecasts seek to foretell. On the face of it, then, with nothing to guarantee correspondence between the actual future and the future as it is envisaged, it might seem as if successful action were entirely a matter of good fortune. Indeed, if man is aware of this apparent lack of ability to envisage the future correctly except as a matter of sheer good fortune, it is not clear why (apart from the joys of gambling

itself) man bothers to act at all. But of course the over-
whelming fact of human history is that man does act, and
his choices are made in terms of an envisaged future that,
although by no means a photographic image of the future
as it will actually unfold, is yet not entirely without
moorings in regard to that realized future. "To be genuine, choice must be neither random nor predetermined.
There must be some grounds for choosing, but they must
be inadequate; there must be some possibility of predicting the consequences of choice, but none of perfect prediction."[30] "The essence of the situation is action according to *opinion*, . . . neither entire ignorance nor complete
and perfect information, but partial knowledge."[31] The
genuine choices that do, I am convinced, make up human
history express man's conviction that the future as he envisages it does hold correspondence, in some degree, to
the future as it will in fact unfold. The uncertainty of the
future reflects man's awareness that this correspondence
is far from complete; the fact that he acts and chooses at
all reflects his conviction that this correspondence is far
from negligible. Whence does this correspondence, incomplete though it may be, arise? If there are no constraints assuring correspondence, how is successful
action anything but the sheerest good fortune?

The answer to this dilemma surely lies in the circumstance that man is *motivated* to formulate the future
as he envisages it, as accurately as possible. It is not a
matter of two unfolding tapestries, one the realized future, the second a fantasized series of pictures of what the
first might look like. Rather, acting man really does try to
construct his picture of the future to correspond to the
truth as it will be realized. He really does try to glimpse
the future, to peer through the fog. He is thus motivated
to bring about correspondence between the envisaged and
the realized futures. Not only are man's purposeful efforts
to better his condition responsible for his choices as constructed against a given envisaged future, that pur-
posefulness is, perhaps even more importantly, respon-

sible for the remarkable circumstance that that envisaged future does overlap significantly with the future as it actually unfolds. (Of course, these forecasts need not be made, explicitly, prior to action; they are embedded, possibly without self-awareness, in action itself.) I call this motivated propensity of man to formulate an image of the future man's *alertness*. Were man totally lacking in alertness, he could not act at all: his blindness to the future would rob him of any framework for action. (In fact, were man totally lacking in potential for alertness, it would be difficult to identify a notion of error altogether: were unalert man to act, it would not be on the basis of an erroneously forecast future. It would be on the basis of no relevant forecast at all. Not recognizing that he might— had he been more alert—have avoided the incorrect picture of the future, he could not in any meaningful sense blame himself for having erred.)

It will surely be acknowledged that this alertness— which provides the only pressure to constrain man's envisaged future toward some correspondence with the future to be realized—is what we are searching for under the phrase "the entrepreneurial element in human action." Robbinsian allocation activity contains no such element, because within the assigned scope of such defined activity no possible divergence between a future as envisaged and a future to be realized is considered. What is incomplete in the notion of purely allocative activity is surely to be found precisely in this abstraction from the desperately important element of entrepreneurship in human action.

It should be observed that the entrepreneurial alertness we have identified does not consist merely in "seeing" the unfolding of the tapestry of the future in the sense of seeing a preordained flow of events. Alertness must, importantly, embrace the awareness of the ways the human agent can, by imaginative, bold leaps of faith, and determination, in fact *create* the future for which his present acts are designed. As I shall argue in a subsequent section, this latter expression of entrepreneurial alertness does not affect its essential formal character—which remains that of ensuring a tendency for the future context envisaged as following present action to bear some realistic resemblance to the future as it will be realized.

In understanding this entrepreneurial element in human action, we must notice, two aspects of it: (1) We note what provides the scope for entrepreneurship. This scope is provided by the complete freedom with which the future as envisaged might, without entrepreneurial alertness, diverge from the future as it will in fact be. Entrepreneurial alertness has a function to perform. (2) We note what provides the incentive that switches on entrepreneurial alertness. This incentive is provided by the lure of pure entrepreneurial profit to be grasped in stepping from a less accurately envisaged future to a more accurately envisaged one. Each step taken in moving toward a vision of the future that overlaps more significantly with the truth is not merely a step toward truth (that is, a positive entrepreneurial success); it is also a profitable step (that is, a step that enhances the value of the resources with which action is available to be taken).

Viewed from this perspective, the tension between the uncertainty environment in which action occurs, on the one hand, and the discovery-of-error aspect of action, on the other, can be seen to dissolve at a glance. These two aspects of action can be seen immediately as merely two sides of the same entrepreneurial coin. If uncertainty were merely an unpleasant condition of life to which man must passively adjust, then it would be reasonable to distinguish between the quite separate activities of bearing uncertainty on the one hand and of discovering error on the other. Escaping from current errors is one thing; grappling with the uncertainty of the future is another. But, as we have noticed, to choose means to *endeavor*, under the incentive to grasp pure profit, to identify a more truthful picture of the future. Dealing with uncertainty is motivated by the profit to be won by avoiding error. In this way of viewing the matter the distinction between escaping current error and avoiding potential future error is unimportant. The discovery of error is an interesting feature of action because it offers incentive. It is this incentive that inspires the effort to pierce the fog of uncertainty that shrouds the future. To deal with uncertainty means to seek to overcome it by more accurate prescience; to discover error is merely that aspect of this endeavor that endows it with incentive attraction. The imagination and creativity with which man limns his envisaged future are inspired by the pure gains to be won in ensuring that that envisaged future is in fact no less bright than that which can be made the truth.

We shall find in the next section that these insights surrounding entrepreneurship at the level of individual action have their exact counterparts in entrepreneurship in the market context. It will be useful to summarize briefly the key points we have learned about individual entrepreneurship:

1. Entrepreneurship in individual action consists in the endeavor to secure greater correspondence between the individual's future as he envisages it and his future as it will in fact unfold. This endeavor consists in the individual's alertness to whatever can provide clues to the future. This alertness, broadly conceived, embraces those aspects of imagination and creativity through which the individual may himself *ensure* that his envisaged future will be realized.

2. Scope for entrepreneurship is provided by the uncertainty of the future. For our purposes uncertainty means that, in the absence of entrepreneurial alertness, an individual's view of the future may diverge with total freedom from the realized future. In the absence of entrepreneurial alertness it is only sheer chance that can be responsible for successful action.

3. Incentive for the "switching on" of entrepreneurial alertness is provided by the pure gain (or avoidance of loss) to be derived from replacing action based on

less accurate prescience by action based on the more realistically envisaged future. The avoidance of entrepreneurial error is not merely a matter of being more truthful, it happens also to be profitable.

Entrepreneurship in the Market

Our examination of the entrepreneurial element in individual action permits us to see the role of entrepreneurship in the market in a fresh light. We shall discover, in the market context, elements that correspond precisely to their analogues in the individual context. Let us consider what happens in markets.

In a market, exchanges occur between market participants.[32] In the absence of perfect mutual knowledge, many of the exchanges are inconsistent with one another. Some sales are made at low prices when some buyers are buying at high prices. Some market participants are not buying at all because they are unaware of the possibility of buying at prices low enough to be attractive; some are refraining from selling because they are unaware of the possibility of selling at prices high enough to be attractive. Clearly the actions of these buyers and sellers are, from the perspective of omniscience, uncoordinated and inconsistent. We notice that, although the assumption of perfect knowledge that is necessary for market equilibrium would constrain different transactions in the market to complete mutual consistency, the actuality of imperfect knowledge permits these different transactions in different parts of the market to diverge with apparently complete freedom. What alone tends to introduce a modicum of consistency and coordination into this picture, preventing a situation in which even the slightest degree of coordination could exist only as a matter of sheerest chance, is market entrepreneurship, inspired by the lure or pure market profit. We are now in a position to identify, in the market context, elements that correspond to key features already identified in the context of individual entrepreneurship.

Corresponding to uncertainty as it impinges on individual action, we have market discoordination. The freedom with which an individual's envisaged future may diverge from the future to be realized corresponds precisely to the freedom with which transactions made in one part of the market may diverge from transactions made elsewhere. In the absence of entrepreneurship it is only out of the purest chance that market transactions by different pairs of buyers and sellers are made on anything but the most wildly inconsistent terms. There is nothing that constrains the mutually satisfactory price bargain reached between one pair of traders to bear any specific relation to corresponding bargains reached between other pairs of traders.

Corresponding to error at the level of the individual, we have price divergence at the level of the market. Perfect knowledge (such as in Robbinsian individual allocative activity) precludes error. Market equilibrium (implied by universal perfect knowledge) precludes price divergences.

The individual entrepreneurial element permits the individual to escape from the distressing freedom with which divergences between envisaged futures and realized futures may occur; the entrepreneur fulfills the same function for the market. The function of the entrepreneur is to bring different parts of the market into coordination with each other. The market entrepreneur bridges the gaps in mutual knowledge, gaps that would otherwise permit prices to diverge with complete freedom.

Corresponding to the incentive for individual entrepreneurship provided by more realistic views of the future, we have at the market level the incentive provided by opportunities for pure entrepreneurial profit. Market profit consists in the gap between prices generated by error and market inconsistency—just as the source for private gain is to be discovered in a present divergence between the imagined and the actual future.

The following are propositions, in the context of the market, that concern entrepreneurship; they correspond precisely to those stated at the conclusion of the preceding section.[33]

1°. Entrepreneurship in the market consists in the function of securing greater consistency between different parts of the market. It expresses itself in entrepreneurial alertness to what transactions are in fact available in different parts of the market. It is only such alertness that is responsible for any tendency toward keeping these transactions in some kind of mutual consistency.

2°. Scope for market entrepreneurship is provided by the imperfect knowledge that permits market transactions to diverge from what would be a mutually consistent pattern.

3°. Incentive for market entrepreneurial activity is provided by the pure gain to be won by noticing existing divergences between the prices at which market transactions are available in different parts of the market. It is the lure of market profits that inspires entrepreneurial alertness.

Time, Uncertainty, and Entrepreneurship

My analogy between entrepreneurship at the level of the individual and entrepreneurship in the market emphasized only the most salient respects of the analogy. Certain additional features of the entrepreneurial function in the market need to be dealt with more extensively. In the individual context the divergence (which it is the function of entrepreneurship to limit) was a divergence between anticipated and realized future. Its source in uncertainty was immediately apparent. In the market context the divergence (which it is the function of entrepreneurship to limit) was a divergence between the transactions in different parts of the market. Its source was stated in terms of imperfect mutual knowledge among market participants. Its relationship to uncertainty was not asserted. This requires both amplification and modification.

My statements concerning market entrepreneurship were couched in terms of the market for a single commodity within a single period. It should be clear that nothing essential is lost when our picture of the market is expanded to include many commodities and, in particular, the passage of time. This should of course not be understood to mean that the introduction of the passage of time does not open up scope for additional insights. I merely argue that the insights we have gained in the single-period context for entrepreneurship are not to be lost sight of in the far more complex multiperiod case.

When we introduce the passage of time, the dimensions along which mutual ignorance may develop are multiplied. Market participants in one part of today's market not only may be imperfectly aware of the transactions available in another part of that market, they also may be imperfectly aware of the transactions that will be available in next year's market. Absence of consistency between different parts of today's market is seen as a special case of a more general notion of inconsistency that also includes inconsistency between today's transactions and those to be transacted next year. A low price today may be in this sense inconsistent with the high prices that will prevail next year. Scope for market entrepreneurship, in the context of the passage of time, arises then from the need to coordinate markets also across time. Incentive for market entrepreneurship along the intertemporal dimension is provided not by arbitrage profits generated by imperfectly coordinated present markets but, more generally, by the speculative profits generated by the as yet imperfectly coordinated market situations in the sequence of time. And, of course, the

introduction of entrepreneurial activity to coordinate
markets through time introduces, for individual entrepreneurs engaged in market entrepreneurship, precisely the considerations concerning the uncertain future
that we have, until now, considered only in the context of
the isolated individual.

It is because of this last circumstance that we must
acknowledge that the introduction of the passage of time,
although leaving the overall formal function of market
entrepreneurship unchanged, will of course introduce
substantial modification into the way we must imagine
entrepreneurship to be exercised concretely. It is still the
case, as noted, that the entrepreneurial function is that of
bringing about a tendency for transactions in different
parts of the market (conceived broadly now as including
transactions entered into at different times) to be made in
greater mutual consistency. But whereas in the case of
entrepreneurship in the single-period market (that is, the
case of the entrepreneur as arbitrageur) entrepreneurial
alertness meant alertness to present facts, in the case of
multiperiod entrepreneurship alertness must mean alertness to the future. It follows that market entrepreneurship
in the multiperiod case introduces uncertainty as facing
the entrepreneur not only as in the analogy offered in the
preceding section—where the market analogue for uncertainty turned out to be the freedom with which transactions in different parts of today's market may
unconstrainedly diverge from being mutually consistent—but also in the simple sense of the entrepreneur's
awareness of the freedom with which his own envisaged
future (concerning future market transactions) may diverge from the realized future. In particular the futurity that
entrepreneurship must confront introduces the possibility
that the entrepreneur may, by his own creative actions, in
fact *construct* the future as *he* wishes it to be. In the single-
period case alertness can at best discover hitherto overlooked current facts. In the multiperiod case entrepreneurial alertness must include the entrepreneur's

perception of the way creative and imaginative action may vitally shape the kind of transactions that will be entered into in future market periods.

Thus the exercise of entrepreneurial alertness in the multiperiod market context will indeed call for personal and psychological qualifications that were unneeded in the single-period case. To be a successful entrepreneur one must now possess those qualities of vision, boldness, determination, and creativity that we associated earlier with the entrepreneurial element in isolated individual action with respect to an uncertain future. There can be no doubt that in the concrete fulfillment of the entrepreneurial function these psychological and personal qualities are of paramount importance. It is in this sense that so many writers are undoubtedly correct in linking entrepreneurship with the courage and vision necessary to *create* the future in an uncertain world (rather than with merely seeing what stares one in the face).

However, the function of market entrepreneurship in the multiperiod context is nonetheless still that spelled out in the preceding section. What market entrepreneurship accomplishes is a tendency for transactions in different parts of the market (including the market at different dates) to become coordinated. The incentive that inspires this entrepreneurial coordination is the lure of pure profit—the difference in market values resulting from hitherto less complete coordination. These insights remain true for the multiperiod case no less than for the arbitrage case. For some purposes it is no doubt important to draw attention to the concrete psychological requirements on which successful entrepreneurial decision making depends. But for other purposes such emphasis is not required; in fact such emphasis may divert attention from what is, from the perspective of the overall functioning of the market system, surely the essential feature of entrepreneurship: its market-coordinative properties.

Let us recall that at the level of the individual, entrepreneurship involved not merely bearing uncertainty but also overcoming uncertainty. Uncertainty is responsible for what would, in the absence of entrepreneurship, be a failure to perceive the future in a manner sufficiently realistic to permit action. Entrepreneurship, so to speak, pushes aside to some extent the swirling fogs of uncertainty, permitting meaningful action. It is this function of entrepreneurship that must be kept in view when we study the market process. The uncertainty that characterizes the environment within which market entrepreneurship plays its coordinative role must be fully recognized; without it there would be no need and no scope for entrepreneurship. But an understanding of what entrepreneurship accomplishes requires us to recognize not so much the extent to which uncertainty is the ineradicable feature of human existence as the extent to which both individual action and social coordination through the market can occur significantly despite the uncertainty of the future (and in spite also of the uncertainty analogue that would, in the absence of the arbitrageur, fog up even the single-period market).

Further Reflections on Uncertainty and Alertness

Thus we can see how those writers who have denied that the pure entrepreneurial role involves the bearing of uncertainty were both correct and yet at least partly irrelevant. Both J. A. Schumpeter[34] and J. B. Clark insisted that only the capitalist bears the hazards of business; the pure entrepreneur has, by definition, nothing to lose.[35] No doubt all this is true, as far as it goes, but what is important about linking the entrepreneur with the phenomenon of uncertainty is not that it is the entrepreneur who accepts the disutilities associated with the assumption of the hazards of business in an uncertain world. What is important is that the entrepreneur, motivated by the lure of pure profits, attempts to pierce these uncertainties and endeavors to see the truth that will permit profitable action on his part.

A number of economists may be altogether unwilling to accept the notion of alertness with respect to uncertain future. In fact many may wish to reject the very formulation I have employed to schematize the uncertainty of the future. For me uncertainty means the essential freedom with which the envisaged future may diverge from the realized future. Entrepreneurial alertness means the ability to impose constraints on that freedom, so that the entrepreneur's vision of the future may indeed overlap, to some significant extent, with that future he is attempting to see. But many will be unwilling to treat the future as something to be seen at all. "The present is uniquely determined. It can be seen by the eye-witness. . . . What is the future but the void? To call it the future is to concede the presumption that it is already 'existent' and merely waiting to appear. If that is so, if the world is determinist, then it seems idle to speak of choice."[36] Similarly, many are unwilling to see the entrepreneur as "alert to opportunities" if this terminology implies that future opportunities already "exist" and are merely waiting to be grasped. "Entrepreneurial projects are not waiting to be sought out so much as to be thought up."[37]

What perhaps needs to be emphasized once again is that in using phrases such as "grasping future opportunities," "seeing the future correctly or incorrectly," or the "divergence between the envisaged future and the realized future" I do not wish to imply any determinacy regarding the future. No doubt, to say that one sees the future (with greater or lesser accuracy) is to employ a metaphor. No doubt that future that one "sees" is a future that may in fact be constructed significantly by one's action, which is supposed to be informed by that very vision. But surely these metaphors are useful and instructive. To dream realistically in a way that inspires successful, creative action is to "see correctly" as compared with the fantasies that inspire absurd ventures or the cold water poured by the unduly timid pessimist that stunts all efforts at improvement. "The future," we have learned, "is unknowable, though not unimaginable."[38] To acknowledge the unknowability of the future is to acknowledge the essential indeterminacy and uncertainty surrounding human existence. But surely in doing so we need not consign human existence to wholly uncoordinated chaos. To speak of entrepreneurial vision is to draw attention, by use of metaphor, to the formidable and benign coordinative powers of the human imagination. Austrian economists have, in principled fashion, refused to see the world as wholly knowable, as suited to interpretation by models of equilibrium from which uncertainty has been exhausted. It would be most unfortunate if, in pursuing this refusal, economists were to fall into a no less serious kind of error. This error would be the failure to understand how entrepreneurial individual actions, and the systematic market forces set in motion by freedom for entrepreneurial discovery and innovation, harness the human imagination to achieve no less a result than the liberation of mankind from the chaos of complete mutual ignorance. Mises's concept of human action and his analysis of the role of entrepreneurial market processes surely remain, in this regard, unique and as yet insufficiently appreciated contributions to the profound understanding of human society.

FOUR

The Entrepreneurial Process

The term *entrepreneurial process* has come to possess two rather distinct, although interrelated, meanings: The two meanings are (1) the process of entrepreneurial competition responsible, in the short run, for the tendencies for the market price of each commodity or input to move toward the respective market-clearing level, for the array of outputs to reflect the pattern of consumer preferences in the light of currently available technological possibilities, and for pure profit opportunities to be ground down to zero; and (2) the process of entrepreneurial discovery, invention, and innovation through which long-run economic growth is stimulated and nourished. The first kind of entrepreneurial process (short-run) is seen as responsible for a continuous tendency toward economic balance and internal economic consistency. The second (long-run) achieves a continual series of steps that together propel the engine of long-run economic growth and development. The second kind of process is the better known than the first and was perhaps most notably discussed in the work of Joseph Schumpeter.[1] Most of this chapter will be concerned with the entrepreneurial process in a sense closer to the second of these two meanings than to the first. However, it is central to my view that a full understanding of long-term entrepreneurial processes will reveal them to be simply a consistent implication and extension of the short-run processes. Although

Reprinted by permission of the publisher from *The Environment for Entrepreneurship*, edited by Calvin A. Kent (Lexington, Mass.: Lexington Books, D. C. Heath and Company, copyright 1984, D. C. Heath and Company).

Schumpeter himself did not see the long-run entrepreneurial process quite in this way, I shall argue that the Schumpeterian process can be illuminated by an understanding of the first (short-run) entrepreneurial processes. And I shall argue further that in attempting to formulate policy that should encourage (or at least release) the long-run processes of entrepreneurial discovery necessary for vigorous growth, it will be highly useful to bear in mind the linkages that prevail between these long-run and short-run processes. In other words, the way to permit long-run entrepreneurial growth processes to take off is to recognize and encourage the kinds of entrepreneurial discoveries that make up the short-run processes.

The Neglect of Entrepreneurship in Growth Economics

Until quite recently growth economics suffered rather seriously from the neglect of the entrepreneurial role. As Harvey Leibenstein has pointed out, it is one of the "curious aspects of the relationship of neoclassical theory to economic development" that "in the conventional theory, entrepreneurs as they are usually perceived play almost no role."[2] This neglect pervaded not only growth economics but economic analysis in general. It would have been too much to expect an analytical framework that, in regard to markets in general, accorded no special significance to entrepreneurial activity—or in fact any scope for such activity—to analyze growth along entrepreneur-theoretic lines.

As a consequence, conventional thinking about the way economic growth occurs and about the ways it might be enhanced tended to be clouded. Much of the discussion of economic growth and development was, for example, aggregative in tone and approach. The economy was discussed as if it were an integrated economic organism; as if individual decision making by firms, investors, and consumers could be costlessly suppressed insofar as the processes of economic growth were concerned. Certainly no need was recognized for any mutual information among individual participants in the economy.

Moreover, the aggregate economy was seen as rigidly circumscribed by resource scarcity that limited growth possibilities along very definite paths. These scarcity constraints were thought not only to govern the posssibilities in hypothetical market economies, but also to delineate optimal growth patterns. Little awareness was displayed that the objectivity of these constraints disappears as soon as it is realized how heavily dependent they are on the assumption that nothing further can be or is likely to be discovered concerning new and better ways of using given resources, or concerning the existence of hitherto unsuspected resources.

An important ingredient in economic growth was recognized to be the continual availability of improved technology. But technological advance was seen as occurring in an inexorably impersonal manner and to be somehow effortlessly and automatically available to all parts of an economy. In particular, the opportunities for growth were seen as marked out, given initial technology, by a clearly defined array of intertemporal investment possibilities that somehow existed apart from any need for them to be discovered, and whose very existence dictated the appropriate growth path. There was no suggestion that the set of opportunities likely to be in fact discovered might in some way depend on the institutional framework within which growth was sought.

It is therefore hardly surprising to find that this earlier growth and development literature not only failed to explore the policies and institutional patterns that might stimulate profit-motivated individual market entrepreneurship; it in fact tended to take for granted that markets were entirely unnecessary for the achievement of growth and that the naturally preferred mode for growth was through wise central planning.

An Entrepreneurial View
of Economic Development

The view of economic growth and development in this chapter contrasts sharply with that critically described in the preceding section. I will emphasize the *open-endedness* of economic systems. Although I will by no means ignore or deny the prime importance of resource scarcity, either in respect to output at any given date or in regard to the possibilities of increases in output level over time, my emphasis will be on the need and scope for processes of discovery that may in effect render scarcity less overriding in accounting for growth. I will thus be concerned not so much with the ways human beings ensure that every ounce of perceived output possibility is properly exploited as with the incentives to stimulate the perception of possibilities. It is this perception that is responsible for the open-endedness of the economic process. We never know what real possibilities remain to be discovered; we never know what the real limits are to the elasticity of the resource constraints that circumscribe our existence.

In understanding the processes of entrepreneurial discovery that are crucially important for growth, aggregation is a distinct handicap. Treating the economy as a whole and abstracting from the opportunities created by interpersonal error within the system inevitably diverts analytical attention from discovery processes made necessary and possible by such error. Treating growth simply as a phenomenon best achieved through deliberate planning inevitably clamps economic growth into a framework from which open-ended discovery is excluded. To plan is not to discover; in fact to plan presumes that the framework within which planning takes place is already fully discovered. In contrast, I see the unfolding development of a nation's economy over time as a process made up, to a major extent, of the interaction of innumerable individual acts of mutual discovery. An understanding of the institutional climate within which such spontaneous processes of unpredictable mutual discovery can best flourish is central. Let us first examine somewhat more systematically the way entrepreneurial discovery constitutes a unique ingredient in economic growth.

Robinson Crusoe, Entrepreneurship, and Economic Growth

Imagine a "Robinson Crusoe" economy with a low volume of output. We might initially classify the possible reasons for this low level of production (and for Crusoe's consequently low standard of living) in the following manner: (1) Crusoe may command only severely limited resources, thus constraining output to a low level; (2) resources may be available to permit higher levels of output, but these levels are not being attained because of Crusoe's lack of technical knowledge of how to properly utilize the resources available (3) both the resources to permit higher output and the knowledge necessary to harness the resources may be available to Crusoe, but the higher output is not forthcoming because of Crusoe's ignorance of the availability of the resources, the availability of the technical knowledge needed to utilize them, or both. In terms of this array of possible reasons, it is clear that a process of economic development raising the quantity and quality of Crusoe's output may be the result of any or all of the following: an increased endowment of resources (including an increased stock of capital goods, presumably as a result of deliberate saving and investment); an increased command over the technical knowledge needed to exploit available resources; or discovery of the resources and the technical knowledge that are already available.

Now this way of putting matters is obviously awkward. Technical knowledge is no less a resource for Crusoe than is steel, or labor, or land. Changes in the endowment of Crusoe's knowledge need not, it may be objected, be treated separately from changes in his endowments of other resources. This deliberately awkward classification has been, in fact, employed strictly in order to accentuate an important but often missed distinction—between the technical knowledge needed to utilize given physical resources on the one hand and, on the other hand, *the knowledge that resources are in fact available.* Technical knowledge can be treated as a resource; but knowledge of the availability of resources cannot. There is a fundamental difference between the way changes in the stock of technical knowledge may enter into the explanation of economic development, and the way changes in the knowledge of *availability* of resources enter into such explanation.

Economic development based on growth of Crusoe's technical knowledge may be perceived to occur in the same logically understandable manner as development based on expanded physical resources. Expansion of physical resources may, of course, be either planned or unplanned. In the case of unplanned expansion of physical inputs, as for example when unexpected beneficial changes in climate occur, Crusoe enjoys expanded output by simply continuing to exploit available resources to the utmost. In the more important case of planned expansion of inputs, Crusoe may, by deliberately channeling his productive energies to this end, increase the volume and quality of capital goods, thus generating eventual increases in output flows. Economic growth and development, in these cases, follows for Crusoe from the logic of expanded opportunities made possible by the planned or unplanned available volume of resources. Output possibilities are restricted by the scarce available resources; expansion of resources is followed by exploitation of the now expanded volume of output possibilities.

Growth of Crusoe's technical knowledge, quite similarly, expands the range of productive possibilities. What Crusoe can produce today out of given physical resources with today's technical knowledge is greater than what he could produce with the same resources without today's knowledge. The expanded technical knowledge may have been at least partly unplanned (as has occurred on numerous occasions during the history of technology), or more likely it may have come about at least partly as a result of deliberate investment in research. Growth in technical knowledge expands the range of production possibilities, thus providing an immediate explanation for growth in output.

The key point is that in such cases development consists in the exploitation of expanded opportunities. The volume of opportunities grows, hence output grows. A very large part of economic analysis depends on the postulate that an optimal opportunity that exists is an opportunity that is immediately grasped. From this perspective, growth in the availability of Crusoe's resources, whether consisting of physical inputs or technical knowledge, whether as a result of planned investment or fortuitously increased endowment, provides an immediately convincing explanation for growth in output.

Here lies the important distinction, for explanations of development, between growth in technical knowledge on the one hand and an increased awareness of the availability of resources on the other. For where development occurs as a result of increased awareness of the availability of resources, it occurs *not* because of the availability of new opportunities, but because of expanded awareness of existing opportunities. To understand development that has occurred in this way, it is necessary to escape the economist's assumption that an optimal opportunity that exists is an opportunity immediately grasped. It is necessary to recognize that desirable opportunities may go unnoticed and hence unexploited; it is necessary to understand the entrepreneurial process whereby opportunities that were hitherto existent but unseen become opportunities seen and exploited.

Entrepreneurial discovery of existing opportunities

is relevant to an understanding of economic development along two dimensions.

1. At a given point in time output may be less than is possible and desired, because of opportunities that have remained unnoticed. Entrepreneurial discovery of these opportunities makes possible a growth in output.

2. As time goes by, expansion of resources (physical or otherwise, planned or unplanned) expands the range of productive possibilities. For this to be translated into growth in output, it is not enough that these expanded possibilities exist—they must be perceived. Here too entrepreneurial discovery is an indispensable ingredient in economic development.

Markets, Entrepreneurship, and Economic Growth: An Apparent Problem

The foregoing Crusonian discussion may be applied, with appropriate modification, to a certain problem in the analysis of growth in a market context. A correct allocation of resources is one that commits each unit of resource to its most highly valued use. An expansion of available resources is presumed to generate expanded output value because we take it for granted that decision makers will tend to correctly allocate the increased resources. This applies to increased technical knowledge no less than to expanded physical resources. If an available unit, say of a scarce raw material, can be utilized in production somewhere in a competitive economy, its market price will, we are taught, tend to rise toward the value of its marginal product in its best use, ensuring that its owner will tend to find it wasteful not to deploy it in that use. Similarly, if a scrap of scarce technical knowledge can enhance the productivity of physical resources somewhere in the economy, potential users of this knowledge will bid for it until its market price tends to correspond to its highest marginal usefulness. But the same market process does not directly apply to knowledge of the availability of resources or, more generally, to knowledge of value.

Let us imagine that a simple, costless operation linking together two items each valued at $1 can transform them into a product worth $12. Clearly this availability of an opportunity for $10 of pure entrepreneurial profit indicates that market participants in general have not realized that this profitable transformation is feasible, or that it is profitable. The market lacks knowledge of the resources available to create $10 of pure profit. Or we may say that the market lacks the knowledge of the true value of the two items of input: the true joint value of these inputs is $12; the market incorrectly believes it to be only $2. Can we, with respect to this missing knowledge, rely on the general market tendency for items to be valued so as to fully reflect their most important uses? Can we assume a tendency for the market to correctly assign full value to this missing knowledge? There are serious logical difficulties involved in any attempt to answer these questions affirmatively.

To assume a tendency for the market to assign full value to the missing knowledge would require that would-be users of this missing knowledge bid for it. That is, we would have to postulate that competing bidders, eager to capture the $10 of profit available through transforming the $2 worth of inputs into $12 of output are prepared to pay for the information that would make such capture possible. This could force up the price of this knowledge of value until it approximates the full $10 that it is capable of generating. But the truth is that we cannot, in this case, assume (as we were able to assume in the case of technical knowledge) that there will be bidders for the missing knowledge.

A moment's reflection should make this clear. Market participants have in general failed to notice that there is a way to transform $2 worth of input into $12 worth of output. In other words, these market participants are not aware that they are overlooking the $10 opportunity of pure profit. Those aware of the inputs place no higher value upon them than $2. Those aware of the high $12 value of the output are aware of no opportunity to achieve such output at an outlay that would make its production available. It is not that market participants feel they lack specific knowledge capable of yielding $10; rather it is that market participants have no inkling that there is anything to be known. In these circumstances we have no right to assume that anyone will be bidding for the knowledge of how to convert the $2 worth of input into $12 worth of output or that potential bidders have any idea of the value of such knowledge.

The source of the $10 profit opportunity resides in the undervaluation by the market of the two inputs, in the existence of unperceived value. The true joint value of the two inputs should be $12; the market values them at $2. The value to any individual of the knowledge of this undervaluation should surely be the full value of the pure profit such knowledge can generate—the full amount of the undervaluation. But, by hypothesis, the market is not aware that any value attaches to knowledge of such undervaluation, since no undervaluation is in fact suspected.

Knowledge of the true value of inputs is thus quite different, in this respect, from technical knowledge. Technical knowledge may be valuable, and potential bidders may assess its value and as a result seek its possession. The knowledge of the true value of inputs may indeed be said to possess value, but this value is of a kind that, by its nature, precludes the possibility of its being able to motivate market participants to deliberately seek it out. *To imagine its being deliberately sought after is to imagine away the source of its value.* The knowledge of value is valuable only if it is not known to be valuable. As soon as the market correctly values the knowledge of value, that correctly assessed value shrinks to zero.

If these conundrums surround the notion of the value of the knowledge of value, then it follows that we cannot rely on competitive market bidding to call forth correct knowledge of value—at least in the way competitive bidding can be relied upon to mobilize productive resources. We cannot, apparently, rely on competitive market bidding to ensure that valuable possibilities will be perceived, that the inputs capable of sustaining these possibilities will be correctly valued. And it is here that we recognize the existence of two distinct avenues along which economic development may proceed: through expansion of opportunities arising through increased availability of resources, or through the discovery of hitherto unperceived opportunities. In practice both strands of developmental causation are intertwined. In order for resources to expand, newly possible opportunities must first be perceived.

These two lines of development differ in important ways, however. Where development occurs through the expansion of opportunities, it may be the outcome of a deliberate planning process to expand the volume of resources through investment in human resources or in physical capital goods. The possibility of such a deliberate planning process permits economic development to be understood as the smooth unfolding of a designed growth path. But with respect to that line of development which arises from the flow of discovery of existing opportunities, no such smooth unfolding of designed growth can be identified. It is impossible to deliberately plan a series of discoveries. Just as we cannot imagine an opportunity being deliberately overlooked unless because of some significant cost of deliberate search that in fact renders the opportunity less than worthwhile after all, so too we cannot imagine a systematic plan to notice that which has hitherto been overlooked. All this means that economic development requires, as part of its explanation, understanding of the entrepreneurial element and of the way this element eludes the analytical tools of standard economic theory.

Allocation, Growth, and Entrepreneurship

A good deal of modern economics is concerned with the forces that determine the allocation of society's resources among alternative production possibilities. There were times, in the past at least, when professional economic discussion seemed to draw a sharp distinction between the allocative function of economic systems on the one hand and the process of economic growth on the other. It was as if economic growth presented a series of problems and tasks to which allocative considerations were totally irrelevant. Thus, for example, economists who expressed full confidence in the capacity of markets to allocate society's resources with reasonable efficiency were quick to deny any similar ability of markets to achieve a desirable rate of growth for the economy.[3] The allocative properties of markets apparently failed to include, as an implication, the capacity to successfully lift the total volume of output over time. To use existing resources efficiently called for deploying these resources to avoid waste. To achieve growth, it was held, called for the fulfillment of a quite different task: the steady increase of the total volume of these resources.

This dichotomy appears flawed in several somewhat subtle respects, though it does, of course, possess a certain superficial plausibility. An increase in the total volume of resources available to society is after all not the same as a more effective utilization of the resource volume given at a particular date. Indeed, a case can emphatically be made that to increase the total volume of resources calls for qualities—of an entrepreneurial character—unrelated to those required for calculative, optimizing, allocative activity.

That a market can successfully stimulate the efficient allocation of resources is no guarantee that it can perform similarly with respect to the entrepreneurial activity required for growth. If the economists referred to had wished to draw attention to these important distinctions, there would have been far less the critic could quibble over. Unfortunately this was decidedly not the case. As mentioned earlier, for a long time economists discussing growth virtually ignored entrepreneurship. And for a world in which entrepreneurship in the discovery of new resources (or in the discovery of new uses for already known and available resources) is seen as having no scope, the distinction between allocation and growth is deeply flawed.

In a world of given resources (with no scope for any addition to these resources that might arise from discovery) it should be obvious that growth necessarily arises from a particular (intertemporal) pattern of resource allocation. In exactly the same way that efficient allocation of resources is required in order to ensure that society's scarce resources are directed to the particular basket of current consumption goods judged most urgently required, efficient intertemporal allocation of resources is required in order to express any preference rankings that place higher future levels of well-being above currently higher levels of well-being. Economic growth, in a world of given resources, depends strictly on the rate at which consumption enjoyments are postposed to permit capital resources to be built up or new technological knowledge to be acquired.

There seems little basis to postulate any analytical distinction between allocation processes as they relate to alternative current uses of resources on the one hand and allocation procedures as they relate to alternative temporal production possibilities on the other. It is not at all obvious why a market system acknowledged to achieve effective patterns of resource allocation in the first of these senses should be held incapable of achieving comparably efficient intertemporal allocative patterns.

The sharp dichotomy that seemed to be drawn between economic allocation of resources and economic growth was flawed in a rather more complicated sense as well. It is not merely that economic growth turns out to be merely a special case of the more general allocation problem. As soon as scope for entrepreneurial discovery is acknowledged in the context of economic growth, such scope must be acknowledged in the context of short-run resource allocation as well. Thus, although it appeared, in a world without entrepreneurship, as if allocation economics necessarily embraced—indeed, swallowed up— the economics of growth, almost the opposite seems to occur as soon as the role of entrepreneurial discovery is recognized. As soon as the economics of growth becomes correctly viewed as being in large part the economics of entrepreneurial discovery, it becomes difficult to see the processes of short-run resource allocation as anything but special cases of the more general discovery processes that constitute economic growth.

From this latter perspective, then, the allocation/growth dichotomy is flawed not so much because it overlooks the allocative aspects of economic growth as because it tends to reinforce the neglect of the role of entrepreneurship in both short-run and long-run economic processes.

Opportunities, Alertness, and Economic Processes

For an analytical perspective in which entrepreneurship and its role are seen as essential elements, the centrality of allocation is highly questionable. Neither at the level of the analysis of the individual economic decision nor at that level concerned with understanding how society's resources are allocated is it possible to proceed without transcending the allocation schema within which economics has so frequently been constrained.[4] Despite the enormously valuable clarity introduced into modern economics by Lord Robbins's formulation (in which economics was rigidly identified as concerned with the consequences of human allocative behavior and which led to the popular notion of economics as being concerned with the ways societies do and should allocate their scarce resources),[5] the truth is that economics can no longer make do with this rather narrow conception of its nature and concerns.

Economists can no longer take it for granted that individual decision makers, or groups, engage in nothing more than allocative decisions against the background of clearly perceived alternatives. Economists must consider that economic processes, and especially market processes, have a profound impact upon the way individuals perceive the options available to them, while the accuracy and sensitivity of opportunity perception itself crucially affects the nature of these economic and market processes that they set in motion. In other words, economic analysis must grapple with the inescapable entrepreneurial element in action and in society.

Individual action is not seen as merely the calculation of the optimum position relevant to a given set of data; it is seen as an attempt to grasp opportunities that the human agent, peering through a fog of uncertainty, judges to be available. The interaction of decisions in markets is not seen as an instantaneous meshing of plans in which the pattern of calculated optima for the participants is such as to permit all of them to be simultaneously sustained. Rather it is seen as an unrestrained, but by no means haphazard, process in which the opportunities perceived to be available are those that have been overlooked by others. In the face of ceaseless and unpredictable exogenous change, the continual pursuit of as yet unperceived opportunities keeps perceptions from straying too far from reality. The role of entrepreneurial alertness in this sequence deserves to be briefly elaborated.

Entrepreneurial theory labors under what appears to be a serious handicap: the specific outcome selected in any particular entrepreneurial decision cannot, even in principle, be predicted.[6] In contrast, the choice made in the course of allocative decision making is, in microeconomic analysis, viewed as emerging errorlessly and ineluctably from the interaction between the agent's objective function and resource and technological constraints. Economic science can, in the case of the allocative decision, claim to account precisely for the action decided upon. But such can certainly not be claimed for the entrepreneurial decision, in which the agent must determine what he or she believes is the relevant environment within which a course of action must be taken.

Economic science is unable to account precisely for the outcome of such entrepreneurial determination. (It should also be pointed out that the purely allocative decision never does occur, and that in fact it is sheer illusion to imagine that economic science can ever provide the kind of precision suggested in microeconomics textbooks.) Yet it is important not to conclude that, simply because the application of the theory of constrained optimization is insufficient to yield precise outcomes, entrepreneurial decision making and the market processes set in motion by such decisions are entirely without guidance.

The truth is that all human decision making is guided by an extremely powerful force—the motivation to see relevant facts as they are.[7] This pervasive pressure to avoid error and to learn from mistakes operates in ways that are far from being fully known. But this powerful instinct is responsible for whatever success humanity has achieved in coping with its environment. To be human is not merely to calculate correctly within an already perceived environment; it is to be able, by peering into a murky present and an even murkier future, to obtain a reasonably useful grasp of one's true situation.

In the market context a correct perception of one's situation calls for a perception not only of physical possibilities and constraints, but also of the possibilities and constraints imposed by the actions, present and prospective, of others. The market process consists of a sequence of entrepreneurial decisions, each of which, being only partially correct in anticipating the decisions of others, leaves room and incentive for further mutual discovery. Were such decisions made haphazardly, there would be no basis for claiming the existence of systematic entrepreneurial market processes. Such systematic processes of entrepreneurial discovery are based on the determined, purposeful alertness of market participants.

Types of Entrepreneurial Activity

There are many opportunities for alert entrepreneurs. Some are of relevance only for short-run market processes; others hold relevance for long-run processes of growth and development. I wll show that, despite the validity of such classification, the nature of entrepreneurial decision making is, at bottom, no different in regard to long-run growth contexts than in regard to short-run contexts.

There appear to be three major types of concrete entrepreneurial activity: arbitrage activity, speculative activity, and innovative activity. *Arbitrage* activity consists of acting upon the discovery of a present discrepancy (net of all delivery costs) between the prices at which a given item can be bought and sold. Such activity involves the discovery of error, since those who sell at the low price are simply unaware of those who buy at the higher price, and vice versa. This discovery constitutes a discovery of an opportunity for pure gain. It is surely the incentive provided by such opportunities that is responsible for the powerful tendency for such arbitrage opportunities to continually disappear. Arbitrage calls for no innovation. In its pure form it calls for no risk bearing and no capital, since buying and selling are simultaneous.

Speculative activity is an arbitrage across time. It is engaged in by the entrepreneur who believes that he or she has discovered a discrepancy (net of all relevant carrying costs and to be revealed through subsequent history) between the prices at which a given item can be bought today and sold in the future. To believe that one has discovered such a price discrepancy is to believe that one has discovered an opportunity for pure gain. There can be no doubt that it is the incentive so provided that inspires entrepreneurs to undertake speculative activity that, if correct, tends to stabilize price over time. Of course such activity is inextricably intertwined with the bearing of uncertainty and also calls for the cooperation of the capitalist to bridge the time gap involved in the speculation. No innovation is required for the activity of the pure speculator.

Innovative activity consists in the creation (for a future more or less distant) of an output, method of production, or organization not hitherto in use. For such activity to be profitable, it will of course be necessary for the innovator to introduce not just any innovation, but one that displays the very same pattern of intertemporal price discrepancy that is identified with speculative activity. Innovative activity, like speculative activity, retains important parallels with the case of pure arbitrage. Innovation calls for the discovery of an intertemporal opportunity that cannot, even in principle, be said to actually exist before the innovation has been created. To talk of the existence of an undiscovered opportunity for an as yet uncreated innovation is merely to engage in metaphor, although it should be pointed out that in important cases the use of such metaphor may be highly instructive.[8] Nonetheless, innovative activity too can bridge a gap between two markets across time, overcoming what at least from a later perspective can be seen to have been error, inspired by the opportunity to grasp the pure gain set up by the relevant price discrepancy.

Alertness is a concept sufficiently elastic to cover not only the perception of existing arbitrage opportunities, but also the perception of intertemporal speculative opportunities that can be definitively realized only after the lapse of time, and even also the perception of intertemporal opportunities that call for creative and imaginative innovation. Certainly the concrete manifestation of successful speculative (or of innovative) activity may call for personal and psychological qualities substantially different from those needed to engage in pure arbitrage.

Yet the parallelism among the various kinds of entrepreneurial activity remains. All of them consist of taking advantage of price differentials; all are inspired by the pure profit incentive constituted by the respective price differentials; all are made possible by less competent entrepreneurial activity (the errors of others). In other words, all of them involve *knowledge of value*—with all its attendant conundrums discussed earlier. It is the commonality expressed in these parallels, and in this shared link to the elusive knowledge of value, that I wish to emphasize here.

Incentives, Competition, and Freedom of Entry

A feature common to all kinds of entrepreneurial discovery is the incentive of pure profit, arising out of the respective price discrepancies of which the entrepreneurial opportunities consist.[9] It should be emphasized that this is an incentive rather different from the notion of an incentive in the nonentrepreneurial context. In the nonentrepreneurial context incentives are called for to motivate an agent to engage in some *costly* activity. To provide such an incentive is therefore to arrange that the gross payoff from the relevant activity to the agent be seen to be more than sufficient to offset the associated cost sacrifice. To provide an incentive for a laborer to work is to arrange a wage payment that will prove more attractive to the laborer than, for example, the leisure alternative.

In the context of entrepreneurial opportunities, however, the notion of an incentive is quite different. Incentive in this case is for the discovery of an opportunity for net gain. Were the opportunity already perceived, no further incentive would be required to persuade the agent to exploit it. However little we know about the ways different entrepreneurs discover what they discover, almost all such discoveries would not be made were there not the possibility of personally attractive, desirable outcomes.

For the sequence of entrepreneurial discoveries that constitutes the market process, the system of incentives is spiced and sharpened by the awareness that market opportunities are to be found only where they have been overlooked by others. It is here that entrepreneurial incentives and the conditions required for dynamically competitive markets intersect crucially and fruitfully.

It is now fairly well understood that the dynamic competition upon which market systems rely for their effectiveness calls for only one basic prerequisite—freedom of entry.[10] If incumbent firms are aware that others are free to enter whenever they sense an opportunity for profit, this causes incumbents to concentrate on discovering yet more effective ways of efficiently serving the consumer. This means that the entrepreneurial discovery of better ways of serving the consumer is spurred both by the incentives provided to nonincumbents by their perception of as yet unexploited pure profit opportunities and by the incentives provided to incumbents by the threat of losses that may ensue from the entry of competing entrepreneurs. I will now consider the rather limited public policy implications of the insights into the entrepreneurial process developed thus far in this chapter.

The Entrepreneurial Process and Public Policy

The entrepreneurial process is a continuous, endless process of discovery. The opportunities for discovery embrace both those consisting of the discovery of errors by others trading (or expected to trade) in markets now or in the future and the discovery of unsuspected resources or technical feasibilities that constitute genuine innovation.

The solution to society's economic problem (identified by F. A. Hayek as that of the coordination and mobilization of scattered scraps of information) calls for a steady series of successful discoveries. Moreover, once the possibility for discovery is introduced it becomes increasingly apparent that Hayek's coordination problem can, in principle, be extended to cover the opportunities for innovation as well.[11]

> The current price of natural gas and the current level of its consumption may be fully coordinated with one another and with other current prices and market activities (informed by the most up-to-date intelligence). Yet this price may be "too high" and consumption "too low" from the perspective (that may, in several years, be provided by technological or other discoveries) of the possibilities, say of tapping solar energy.[12]

If society has a stake in encouraging the solution to Hayek's coordination problem, this must surely extend to the intertemporal coordination opportunities that can be exploited only by innovative, entrepreneurial breakthroughs. How can society achieve this? What policies can, without incurring unacceptable costs, stimulate or release the potential for discovery that exists in all motivated human beings that make up a society's population?

It should be clear that stimulating the potential for discovery must be a task rather different from that of stimulating or coaxing out a greater supply of a given scarce resource or service. The potential availability of a given scarce resource is usually treated by economists as capable of being expressed by a supply curve. Such a curve relates various potentially available quantities of the resource to the resource prices capable of eliciting these quantities. To command larger available quantities, such a supply curve generally reports, it will be necessary to offer more attractive resource prices. With respect to entrepreneurial talent, however, we are not able to discourse in this fashion. The knowledge of value is never an item deliberately sought after. Nor do those possessing the knowledge of value consciously treat it as a deployable or salable resource.

It is simply not useful to treat entrepreneurship in terms of a supply curve. The exercise of specific quantities of entrepreneurship involves no identifiable cost or required amounts. Yet it is impossible to treat the degree of entrepreneurial discovery prevailing in a society as totally unrelated to public policy. There are two separate ways policy may in principle affect the emergence of entrepreneurial discovery. The first relates to policy that may affect the entrepreneurial attitudes and character of a population. The second relates to policy that may, with a population of given entrepreneurial attitude, stimulate it to be more alert to entrepreneurial opportunities. Arthur Seldon has remarked that the qualities that make for entrepreneurial alertness (such as restive temperament, thirst for adventure, ambition, and imagination) may be nurtured or suppressed. "They are presumably similar in Germany on both sides of the Iron Curtain, in Korea North and South of the 38th parallel, on both sides of the China Sea separating the Chinese mainland from the island of Taiwan, but the results are very different according to the institutions created by government."[13]

Other authors emphasize both access to profit opportunities and security of property rights. The opportunity to obtain profit is by itself not yet sufficient for the emergence of entrepreneurial activity. "The entrepreneur must also be reasonably assured that he may keep entrepreneurial profits that he legitimately acquires. Thus certain institutional practices in a market economy will tend to encourage a high level of entrepreneurial activity, especially (1) a free and open economy that permits equal access to entrepreneurial opportunities, (2) guarantees of ownership in property legally acquired, and (3) stability of institutional practices that establish points 1 and 2"[14] Let us see further what these two kinds of policy goals in-

volve and what, if anything, can be concretely proposed
toward their implementation.

NURTURING THE ENTREPRENEURIAL SPIRIT

Seldon's references to the Iron Curtain, the thirty-
eighth parallel, and the China Sea on the one hand express a conviction that the profound institutional differences that relate to the areas separated by these
boundaries have much to do with nurturing or suppress-
ing the thirst for adventure, ambition, and imagination.
On the other hand, these references reflect a willingness
to recognize the possibility, at least, that ethnic and geo-
graphical factors may be important in determining the extent to which a population displays an entrepreneurial
attitude.

It should be apparent that in regard to the ways geo-
graphic and ethnic factors do or do not affect entrepreneurial spirit our knowledge is woefully meager.
Moreover, research effort applied to these questions has
been extremely limited. Nonetheless a beginning has
been made. Interesting work has, for example, been done
by Benjamin Gilad in bringing to bear existing studies
that point to a relationship between alternative institutional and cultural environments—particularly as these
impinge on the freedom of the individual—and human
qualities germane to the entrepreneurial attitude.[15] It remains to be seen whether further research in this area
strengthens the insights so far suggested and whether
such results offer ideas capable of being translated into
meaningful public policy proposals. It is nonetheless
worth noting that the conclusions to which Gilad's work
points—that economic growth may depend upon the
stimulus to the entrepreneurial spirit supplied by an environment of economic freedom—run precisely counter
to that implied by earlier economists, who saw economic
growth as requiring economic regimentation.[16]

STIMULATING ALERTNESS

Research into techniques of stimulating the alertness of a given group of persons is fragmentary and unsystematic.[17] Many discussions of entrepreneurial alertness have relied on the "plain, unremarkable statement of a fundamental facet of human nature" *that human beings tend to notice what it is their interest to notice.*[18] The social significance of a market system does not reside in the beauty of the allocation pattern under equilibrium conditions. Rather, it rests upon the capacity of markets to translate the errors made in the immediate past into opportunities for pure entrepreneurial profit of direct interest to potential entrepreneurs. Features of the institutional landscape that strengthen the linkage between socially significant opportunities and the likelihood and security of associated entrepreneurial gain (such as those proposed by Hébert and Link, note 14 this chapter) clearly improve the chances for entrepreneurial discovery. The linkage between dynamic competition and entrepreneurship is of direct relevance here. The incentives provided by freedom of entrepreneurial entry, as they act on incumbent entrepreneurs and potential entrants, are relevant in devising ways to stimulate entrepreneurial alertness and discovery.

The Danger of Taking the Entrepreneur for Granted

Perhaps the most important contribution that the recent renewal of professional interest in the entrepreneurial process can make toward public policy is to stimulate a general awareness of the grave dangers that accrue from the error of taking the entrepreneur and his role for granted. No doubt there were eras in the history of the development of economic understanding when this kind of error was relatively less critical. No doubt an understanding of the general pattern of results produced by the entrepreneurial process was more important, for such eras, than an understanding of that process itself. But to make the error of imagining that there really is nothing for entrepreneurs to do, that economic processes are somehow propelled without the entrepreneurial spirit and genius for discovery, is to fall prey to a way of thinking that can harmfully affect social policy. To take the entrepreneur for granted is to overlook the dangers of regulatory or fiscal or antitrust policies that block or discourage entrepreneurial entry into perceived avenues for profitable activity. The entrepreneurial spirit, the potential for discovery, is always waiting to be released. Human ingenuity is irrepressible and perennial, and its release requires an environment free from special privileges or blockages of new entrants. For the successful allocative functioning of the market, and for the stimulation of dynamic growth, the entrepreneur must not be taken for granted.

FIVE

Taxes and Discovery: An Entrepreneurial Perspective

The central theme of this paper will take the form of a rather basic criticism of an unstated premise of the accepted theory dealing with the economic effects of taxation. If this criticism is accepted as sound, it will raise serious questions concerning the completeness (if not the very validity) of the conclusions arrived at through application of the standard theory. In order to reformulate the theory of taxation to take adequate account of our basic criticism, a significant array of new theoretical challenges will have to be grappled with. Thus this paper implies not only a broad attack on orthodox taxation theory, but also an extensive positive agenda for its reconstruction. But it by no means attempts to undertake these formidable tasks. (In fact it must be freely confessed that it is not clear that economics yet possesses the conceptual and analytical tools necessary for these tasks.) It confines itself to the far more modest (and, I hope, achievable) objective of articulating the basic insight underlying my criticism and of identifying some of the theoretical issues that are raised by awareness of this basic insight.

The Premise of Orthodox Theory

Underlying the standard theory that assesses the economic consequences of taxation is the premise *that taxes are introduced into a world in which available op-*

This paper is reprinted from a chapter in *Taxation and Capital Markets*, ed. Dwight R. Lee. Copyright 1985 by the Pacific Institute for Public Policy Research, 177 Post Street, San Francisco, CA 94108.

portunities for gainful actions are given and known (in the sense to be defined below) to relevant decision makers. Acceptance of this premise has meant that the economic impact of a tax is explored only insofar as it may affect the relative preferability for the decision maker of already-perceived alternative courses of action (the fully known benefits of which may be affected unequally by the tax). No consideration is given to the possibility that the tax may have, perhaps, significant impact upon the very perception by the prospective taxpayer of what array of opportunities are available for his choice, or of what their pretax benefits for him may in fact be. In other words, no consideration is given to the possibility that taxation may affect what it is that decision makers *discover* to be the situation in which they act. The effect of taxation upon incentives has been explored on the premise that the degree to which the taxpayer can successfully discover the true state of affairs surrounding him is left unaffected by all taxation patterns (and it is often assumed, in fact, that the taxpayer is able to discover this state of affairs with *complete* success in all circumstances). I shall argue that this basic premise is likely to be, in general, unfounded. Once the possibility is recognized of there being a linkage between what a person is to be taxed and what opportunities that person discovers to be available for his taking, we must recognize further the need to modify substantially the conclusions reached by standard theory (on the basis of this challenged premise) concerning the effect of specific taxes upon what prospective taxpayers decide to do. Let me elaborate briefly on two quite different senses in which the notion of *incentives* may be relevant to the economic analysis of taxation.

Incentives and Incentives

Ordinarily economists treat the concept of an incentive as referring to the provision of an encouragement for a decision maker to select a particular one out of an array of *already perceived alternatives*. What is already perceived about these alternatives is taken to be not only the possible courses of action themselves, but also key elements, at the very least, concerning the respective consequences that can reasonably be expected to follow from pursuing these courses of action. To provide an incentive to encourage the decision maker to select course of action *A*, rather than courses of action *B*, *C*, . . . , means to seek to modify the consequence of these various courses of action in such a manner as to render the perceived consequences of *A* more desirable than those of *B*, *C*, ... Typically this is likely to take the form of arranging an enhancement of the value to the decision maker of the perceived consequence of *A* itself. In other words, the way to induce the decision maker to adopt course of action *A* is, to use the economists' opportunity-cost phraseology, to overcome the cost of sacrificing *B*, *C*, ... Whereas, absent this inducement, course of action *B* might have been judged to promise greater rewards than action *A*, the provided incentive (enhancing the total value of *A*'s consequences) renders *A* more desirable than *B*. The high cost of rejecting *B* has been met by increasing the payoff on action *A*. It is easy to understand how taxes (and subsidies) may be deployed in this way to provide the incentives designed to encourage taxpayers to pursue courses of action which the taxing authorities would like them to pursue.

To encourage work rather than leisure it may be deemed necessary to increase after-tax labor income (without affecting the desirability of relevant forgone leisure); to encourage saving rather than the immediate consumption of income it may be deemed necessary to offer tax exemptions on that portion of income directed toward saving (while leaving unchanged the severity of the tax bite on other income). These tax measures provide tax-based incentives to encourage work, or saving, through modifying the rewards of working, or saving, in such a way as to outweigh the perceived costs of working, or saving. Let us call this kind of incentive an *incentive of the first kind.* I wish to draw attention to an altogether different notion of an incentive that will be of critical importance for the theme of this paper.

This second, entirely different, incentive concept does not operate by overcoming the cost, to the decision maker, associated with his adoption of the to-be-encouraged option A; it does not operate by enhancing the value of A's consequences so as to make these consequences appear more valuable, all in all, than those of B, C, ... Rather, this second kind of incentive operates to encourage the adoption of A by making A more likely to be *noticed* by the decision maker. In other words, it may be the case that even *without* any new incentives, course of action A may *already* have in fact involved consequences more desirable than those of B, C, . . .—but that his preferred action A, would, in the absence of new incentives, *not* have been adopted *simply because it would have failed to have been noticed as a possibility by the decision maker.* Here the incentive takes the form not of altering the *relative* attractiveness of the payoffs to A, B, C, . . . but of somehow enhancing the potential of course of action A to *attract attention.* There is no need to offer incentives in order to overcome the opportunity cost of rejecting course of action B. A is *already* offering greater rewards than B. Thus, if the authorities, in this situation, wish to structure taxes in order to provide taxpayers with incentives to pursue course of action A, any tax policy generated sweetening, for the taxpayer, of the anticipated value of the consequences of undertaking A does not affect action through the enhancement of the relative desirability of A. Rather, the incentive to undertake A operates, under the specified assumptions, *through its inducement to discover* the possibility and/or the attractiveness of A. I will refer to this kind of incentive as an *incentive of the second kind.*

It should perhaps be pointed out that an inducement

to discover *A* is not at all the same as an inducement *deliberately to undertake the search effort* (involving possibly significant search costs) that might reveal the existence and value of *A*. A decision maker might indeed be convinced that, by the expenditure of a specified degree of search effort, he could locate a superior course of action— but that the cost of the necessary search effort was so high as to make the whole search not worthwhile. And tax authorities might indeed then be able, perhaps, to provide sufficient enhancement of the value of the to-be-searched-for course of action so as to make the expensive search appear worthwhile after all. But *this* kind of inducement to search is evidently no different from any of the incentives of the first kind discussed earlier. This kind of inducement is designed to overcome the costs of undertaking an already perceived course of action, namely, that of deliberately searching for a superior course of action (to be undertaken subsequent to the search). This kind of inducement operates (as do all incentives of the first kind) by enhancing the relative desirability of an already perceived (and already correctly evaluated) course of action (the act of searching). The sense in which incentives of the second kind can be said to serve as inducements for discovery is quite different.

Discovery may be induced by incentives of the second kind, not by rendering an already perceived possibility of costly search worthwhile, but by sparking interest in a possible but hitherto *unnoticed* course of action (or at least a course of action whose net desirability had not been noticed). One cannot deliberately search for an opportunity if one is totally unaware of the very possibility of its existence. (One of the avenues through which incentives of the second kind may spark interest in hitherto unnoticed possibilities may of course take the form of sparking interest in the possible worthwhileness of deliberate search itself. But then the reason the search would, absent these new inducements, not have been undertaken deliberately had nothing to do with the costliness of the search effort. The to-be-expected results of a search would, in such cases, be such as to render such cost well worth while; the search would have failed to be undertaken because the very possibility of such a search, or of its likely and valuable successful outcome, was somehow—in the absence of the new incentives—not perceived.)

The theme of this paper can now be concisely stated in terms of the two kinds of incentives described above. This theme is that the standard theory of the economic effects of taxation proceeds exclusively through the analysis of the incentive (or disincentive) effects of taxation in the context of the first kind of incentive concept; what needs to be introduced is an analysis of taxation that takes into account the role of incentives (and disincentives) of the second kind.

The Incentive of Pure Profit

The foregoing suggests rather clearly that the reconstruction of the economic theory of taxation that I am calling for must proceed through a reconsideration of the theory of the economic effects of the taxation of pure entrepreneurial profit. That this is so emerges immediately from the insight that the incentive role of pure profit is entirely that of the *second* kind of incentive discussed in the preceding section. Although the disincentive effects of taxation upon profit have been frequently referred to in the tax literature, it appears that these references have had only the *first* kind of incentive effect in mind. I shall argue in this section that this latter understanding of the incentive effect of profit (and hence of the disincentive effect of profit taxes) is valid only to the extent that accounting profit (upon which taxes may be levied) includes elements other than pure entrepreneurial profit. With respect to the *pure* profit component, I shall maintain, the *only* relevant incentive category is that which I have labeled the second kind.

Pure profit is captured by the entrepreneur when he succeeds in selling an item (a good or a service) at a price that exceeds the price for which he purchased that item (or the total of the outlays incurred in producing that item and making it ready for sale). Pursuing this definition, we observe that all payments necessary to command the services of relevant productive factors have already been included in the outlay total to be subtracted from the sales proceeds in arriving at the pure profit that has been won. By definition, therefore, pure profit is a sum that cannot be described as necessary for the production of the item sold (or for its availability for sale at the relevant selling price). Pure profit contains no element needed to ensure the availability of the item to be sold. All necessary costs of production, including all outlays (such as selling costs, delivery costs, and the like) needed to ensure that the item to be sold will be forthcoming at the appropriate time and place are included in the total deducted from sales revenues in arriving at the profit amount. Pure profits are not needed to provide the economic incentives necessary to evoke relevant productive effort. Notice that this means, of course, that even without the presence of pure profits, sales revenues are, by being sufficient to cover all the necessary factor service outlays, sufficient to overcome the pull exercised by the bids of entrepreneurs in other industries, competing to secure the services of these factors for other productive uses. Any incentive role that may be ascribed to pure profit can therefore not take the form of the first kind of incentive role identified earlier (in which an income receipt provides the incentive to the decision maker to undertake a given course of action by rendering the consequences of that course of action preferable to those of alternate courses of action). Here the course of production action (undertaken in the profitable line of production) would, we have seen, have been worth adopting even if the pure profit amount was not forthcoming from the sales revenues. The possibility that pure profit fulfills an incentive role can therefore exist only in the *second* of the senses I identified earlier (in which an income receipt provides the incentive for a course of action to be undertaken by enhancing the potential of that course of action, and of its worthwhileness, to attract entrepreneurial attention).

That this indeed may be an incentive role provided by pure entrepreneurial profit follows from the very concept of entrepreneurship and from the theory of pure entrepreneurial profit. The very possibility of the emergence of pure entrepreneurial profit rests, after all, on the circumstance that worthwhile opportunities may simply not be noticed. Were all worthwhile opportunities to be noticed at all times (i.e., were all opportunities for producing items whose prospective sales revenues fully covered necessary costs of production to be immediately noticed), then we could hardly expect that sales revenues would ever exceed costs of production. No buyer would pay for an item a sum larger than the perceived minimum outlay sufficient to obtain the availability of that item. The possibility of sales revenue's exceeding cost of production arises solely out of the possibility that desirable courses of action may not be noticed (or that their desirability may not be noticed).

Thus the incentive role of pure entrepreneurial profit fits naturally into the theory accounting for its very existence. Profit is generated by earlier failure of market participants to notice worthwhile possibilities. The profit thus generated sparks interest in these overlooked possibilities. The incentive of profit thus works not to affect the relative attractiveness of already perceived opportunities, but to attract notice to the most desirable (but possibly not yet perceived) of the existing opportunities. The concept of entrepreneurship is closely linked to that of alertly noticing hitherto unnoticed opportunities. As we shall see, there is every reason to recognize the possibility of pure profit as providing the incentive that inspires entrepreneurial discovery of such hitherto unnoticed opportunities. These insights certainly hold considerable relevance for understanding the impact of profit taxation.

I note, in concluding this section, that accounting profit may, of course, not conform at all closely to the pure entrepreneurial profit I have been discussing here. As is well known, accounting profit figures may contain very significant components of a variety of different analytical categories, especially interest and wages of management. To the extent that interest must be paid in order to compete for capital with other branches of production or to dissuade potential investors from succumbing to the lure of more immediate consumption possibilities, or to the extent that wages of management must be paid in order to attract talent away from other pursuits, accounting profits may well be needed to secure the availability of the resource services for this branch of production as against competing branches. To this extent accounting profits may certainly be held to perform the first kind of incentive role identified earlier. The effects of the taxation of accounting profit must certainly deal, as standard theory does, with the *first* kind of disincentive effect of such taxation. (My contention is that such analysis covers only part of the full effects of such taxation.) The discussion in this section has referred *only* to the pure profit element.

At the same time we must not forget that, just as accounting profit is likely to embrace elements other than pure entrepreneurial profit, so also may other accounting categories such as wages, or interest, include elements of pure profit. Let me elaborate briefly on this theme.

The Ubiquity of Pure Profit

I have argued that the reconstruction of the theory of taxation called for in this paper must proceed by way of a reconsideration of the economic effects of the taxation of pure entrepreneurial profit. This does not mean, however, that such reconstruction would leave unaffected the theory dealing with the effects of the taxation of income categories other than accounting profit. The truth of that pure entrepreneurial profit is a ubiquitous economic phenomenon, present in a variety of economic circumstances and captured by a variety of economic agents. As Ludwig von Mises wrote, "In any real and living economy every actor is always an entrepreneur."[1]

What this means is that every action in the market economy reflects the actor's alertness to aspects of his situation that might otherwise have escaped attention. In a changing, open-ended world, acting man is never exempt from the self-generated pressure to ensure that his decisions not overlook available opportunities. Action never does consist merely in selecting the highest valued of a given array of opportunities; it always embraces the simultaneous *identification* of what the relevant opportunities (and their values) really are at the moment of action. While we usually think of pure entrepreneurial profit as generated by the independent businessman through acts of purchase and sale, the truth surely is that an element of profit is captured whenever, say, a worker moves out of an industry where his marginal productivity and therefore his wages are low and obtains a job in another industry or location where compensation for similar skills is higher. This wage differential is the incentive that attracts the worker to change jobs; it can hardly be described as an incentive of the first kind—only a small fraction of it may be needed to render the new job more attractive than the old. Clearly the wage differential acts as an incentive for workers to become alert to the most desirable employment opportunities, in exactly the same way as price differentials attract potential entrepreneurs to buy at low prices and sell at higher prices. The role of incentives of the *second* kind (as I have called them in this paper) is a ubiquitous one. Thus the reconsideration of the economic theory of taxation that I call for in this paper is by no means confined to taxes explicitly levied on profit receipts. The reconstruction and the reconsideration I call for have implications that extend to most kinds of taxes, to greater or lesser degree.

Nonetheless, having recognized the entrepreneurial element in all human action, and having asserted the possibility that incentives of the second kind play roles in almost every kind of economic receipt, we must acknowledge that the adviser on tax policy can hardly be the purist the present section might appear to demand. Assertions concerning the impact of taxation upon analytical categories must, for the purposes of tax policy, be translated into assertions that relate, broadly if not precisely, to empirically identifiable classes of receipts. It is for this reason that most of the subsequent discussion is directed toward the impact of taxation upon accounting profit, insofar as a significant element in it is likely to be pure entrepreneurial profit in the more obvious sense. By "pure profit in the more obvious sense" I mean the difference between the amounts paid and received by an entrepreneur in paired buying and selling transactions (including in the buying transaction the purchase of all factor services needed to make possible a subsequent selling transaction of a produced item).

Pure Profit That Provides No Incentives for Discovery?

I have discussed some of the pitfalls surrounding attempts to identify empirical expressions of the analytical category of pure entrepreneurial profit. The discussion was conducted on the basis of insight into the special character of the incentive provided by pure entrepreneurial profit, namely, that this represents the *second* kind of incentive that I distinguished earlier. It was this insight into the special character of the pure profit incentive that suggested that the impact upon entrepreneurial discovery exercised by the taxation of profit urgently needs to be taken into account. We must now

consider the possibility that the winning of pure entrepreneurial profit—in the form of a surplus of sales revenues over total relevant purchase outlays—may be
accompanied by *no* incentive effects whatever.

This possibility was raised, in a somewhat different
context, by Professor Shackle[2] many years ago. Shackle
distinguished between two possible sources of pure profit: "imagination and knowledge" and "luck." In Shackle's view a goal for tax policy should be to avoid
discouraging the exercise of imagination and knowledge;
but he believed that the taxation of lucky gains involved
no such disincentives. The problem remaining for
Shackle was the practical one: "How are we to determine
when a high rate of profit is due to luck and when to instructed imaginative enterprise?"[3] Only if such a determination can be made is it possible to hope to answer
positively the central questions Shackle poses for tax policy in regard to profit: "Is it possible to devise a form of
tax by which the majority of actual ventures will be
caused to yield some revenue, but which will leave the
incentive to enterprise, that is, the *ex ante* attractiveness
of every venture, entirely unaffected? Can such a tax be so
fashioned that actual gains realized *ex post* are taxed at
lower rates when they accrue to those who have been able
rather than merely lucky?"[4]

Shackle's understanding of the incentive role that
pure profit plays in evoking "instructed imaginative enterprise" on the part of the "able" is perhaps not quite the
same as my interpretation of pure profit as providing incentives "of the second kind." But the questions he has
posed are of direct relevance for our inquiry as well. May
it not, after all, perhaps be the case that a realized difference between sales revenue and purchase outlay corre-
sponded to nothing that provided any incentive (of the
second kind) for discovery but was instead merely the
outcome of a lucky break? To point out that the emergence of pure profit is evidence of hitherto overlooked opportunities is by itself not sufficient to establish that the

entrepreneur who captures such pure profit was inspired to his discovery ex ante by the incentive effect of that prospective profit. May it not, in any particular situation, perhaps be the case that in fact the entrepreneur was the fortunate beneficiary of good luck with nothing at all attributable to his own entrepreneurial alertness? And in addition may it not perhaps be that the nature of the changes that generated the profit margin were so drastic as to have been clearly beyond the scope of possible human anticipation, making it idle to speculate on the incentive power that the prospect of profitability might have had on the entrepreneur's decisions?

If indeed a significant fraction of realized pure profits is to be ascribed to sheer luck and therefore held to have played no incentive role whatever, then much of my concern in this paper would appear to be beside the point. Theorists claiming to account for the consequences of the taxation of profit may well be thought to be responsible to consider the special kind of incentive role (the "second" kind) that pure profit may fulfill in inspiring discovery. But they may be held to be justified in ignoring the second kind of incentive if it turns out that that category of income receipt held to exemplify this second kind of incentive is in fact largely a matter of sheer luck and in no way responsive to, or a result of, "instructed imaginative enterprise." Were we to believe that pure entrepreneurial profit is indeed mainly a matter of sheer good luck, were we to believe that the successful entrepreneur, looking back on his wise decisions, can honestly state that the prospect of the profit eventually grasped played no incentive role in inspiring those decisions—then we would seem to have great difficulty in claiming that the taxation of pure profit operates to discourage alert decision making. And our critique of orthodox taxation theory might seem safe to ignore.

Professor Shackle's own suggestion for distinguishing between lucky profits and profits won through shrewd entrepreneurial judgment, depends heavily on his own ("focus-value") theory of decision making under uncertainty. His suggestion involves the identification of "that one rate of profit which [the entrepreneur] had most vividly in mind when he decided that the venture was sufficiently attractive to warrant his embarking on it."[5] It should be observed that this way of putting the matter makes it clear that the emergence of a profit rate other than the one most "vividly in mind" would be (in Shackle's terminology) the emergence not of an "unexpected" course of events, but of a "counter-expected" course of events.[6] The profit that might emerge would, that is, even if far above that "most vividly in mind," represent an outcome that had at least been considered. Moreover, the framework of Shackle's discussion is one in which "the venture" was one clearly defined, at the moment of decision, quite apart from the rate of profit to be associated with it. The sense in which the vividly anticipated rate of profit served as an incentive to undertake the venture is thus quite different from that I have identified as "incentive of the second kind." Perhaps our appreciation of this difference between Professor Shackle's frame of reference and that developed in this paper may permit us to see the nature of what Professor Shackle considers to be profit due to luck through somewhat different spectacles.

The Counter-Expected and the Unexpected

As we have seen, Shackle identifies a portion of realized pure profit as merely the result of luck, by showing it to have been "counter-expected." Viewing matters from this perspective, it is difficult not to agree with Shackle that the taxation of this portion of profit can have no disincentive effect on enterpreneurial action. But it must be submitted that this understanding of the scope for "imaginative entreprise" sems far too narrow. It may be suggested that a broader view of the entrepreneurial role would permit us to see that what is important is not so much the distinction between the expected (in Shackle's sense of the prospect "most vividly in mind") and the counter-expected, but rather the distinction between what has been considered as a possible contingency and what has somehow not been considered at all. (The latter is what Shackle, p. 73, calls the "unexpected event," i.e., the "contingency which has entirely escaped attention.") This distinction will permit us to recognize the possible incentive character of profit resulting from sheer luck, at several distinct levels.

For me, to choose entrepreneurially calls for more than merely to identify, out of an array of conceivable outcomes perceived as available, what appears most vivid. To choose entrepreneurially must include also the step of "discovering" those courses of action, and those arrays of potential outcomes, that one believes to be relevantly conceivable. Now we know very little about how "incentives of the second kind" operate; we know little about how the attractiveness of an outcome (or an array of possible outcomes) of a course of action stimulates the discovery of the possibility of this course of action. But we do know, if only in a very general way, that potentially attractive outcomes somehow do tend to stimulate attention.[7] We do seem likely to notice what we are personally interested in, more than we are likely to notice what holds no interest for us. From the perspective of our analysis of "incentives of the second kind," we recall that the profit incentive is not called for to stimulate *adoption* of perceived courses of action. Were we to be concerned with what stimulates the entrepreneur *to undertake* a risky, already perceived course of action, we would have to agree that considered but counter-expected outcomes can have played no role in stimulating the relevant assumption of risk by the entrepreneur.[8] Our concern, however, in the context of incentives of the second kind, is with the discovery of possibilities *worthy of considera-tion*. If, say, very attractive potential outcomes help attract attention to a relevant course of action that may be

available, then even if after consideration of this possible
course of action it turns out that *those* outcomes are indeed, in the end, counter-expected—but the course of action is adopted nonetheless because of other more vivid (if
not quite as attractive) outcomes—surely we must concede that those very attractive outcomes have played
their incentive role in the discovery of the adopted course
of action. These insights are already sufficient for us to
recognize that at least some portion of apparently
"lucky" profits (that portion which entrepreneurial fore-
sight had rendered "counter-expected" but not "unexpected") may have played an incentive role in stimulating
adoption of the profitable course of action (by rendering
that course of action sufficiently noticeable to have been
discovered). But we can go even further.

The insights contained in the preceding paragraphs
do not, after all, affect our understanding of profits that
were in fact not merely counter-expected but indeed totally unexpected. Outcomes of an adopted course of action that were so far from the decision maker's field of
vision as to have escaped his notice altogether must surely, even according to these insights, appear to have totally
lacked any incentive role in the fortunate adoption of that
course of action. Yet I shall argue that the distinction between the counter-expected and the unexpected permits,
in the light of my identification of incentives of the second kind, a different view even of this kind of lucky profit. My argument depends on appreciating the *open-ended*
character of the entrepreneurial decision-making context.

Incentives in an Open-Ended World

Although I have made frequent reference to what I
have called "incentives of the second kind" (those that
encourage *discovery* of courses of action, or their desirable outcomes, that might otherwise escape attention), I
have not yet given attention to the paradox inherent in
the very notion of this second kind of incentive. How, one

must surely ask, can an enhancement of the desirability of a particular course of action which by the very definition of this kind of incentive *has not yet been noticed* inspire its discovery? How can an *unnoticed* potential outcome, no matter how attractive, affect behavior? How can the attractiveness of an unknown opportunity that awaits one around the corner possibly inspire one to peer around that corner?

It would be presumptuous and misleading to suggest that I know how to answer these questions. We do not know (and this appears to hold true not only for economists but for psychologists as well) precisely how human beings are inspired by the attractiveness of unknown opportunities. But there can be no doubt that such inspiration has been of enormous importance throughout recorded human history. The sources of the entrepreneurial energy and alertness are still urgently in need of very basic research. Yet we know that the driving force behind this energy and this alertness is firmly rooted in the nature of the unknown—precisely the opposite of the economic motivations that govern nonentrepreneurial endeavor. Ordinary, nonentrepreneurial economic motivation operates within a given (real or assumed), closed set of circumstances. In such circumstances the drive to succeed is motivated by the visible outcomes promised by success, in relation to the perceived necessary sacrifices required by the given, closed framework. The drive that spurs entrepreneurial energy and alertness, on the other hand, appears to have its source in the very openenededness of the entrepreneurial context.

What switches on the entrepreneurial antennae appears to be the potential entrepreneur's awareness that the situation holds unknown possibilities unconstrained by known constraints. It is the entrepreneur's awareness of the *open-endedness* of the decision context that appears to stimulate the qualities of self-reliance, initiative, and discovery.[9] It is here that we encounter once again, in a different context, the distinction between what Professor Shackle called the "counter-expected" and what he called the "unexpected."

What is counter-expected relates to the given, closed decision context. The decision maker knows enough, or at least thinks he knows enough, to be convinced that a considered outcome or event is not to be expected. Even if the counter-expected character of this outcome or event derives from an assessment of the probability of its occurrence (including in the notion of probability any relevant notion of "subjective probability" or of Shackleian potential surprise that one may wish to invoke), the conviction not to expect it resides, in these circumstances, in the set of given constraints viewed as governing the relevant probabilities. To stimulate entrepreneurial alertness, on the other hand, what is needed is the awareness of the *open* character of the situation one is confronting.

From this perspective, the truly unexpected character of an outcome or an event emerges—paradoxically, perhaps—as an aspect of it that is related, possibly in an essential manner, to that which inspires successful entrepreneurial decision making. Entrepreneurial talent consists in peering into an unknown future and arriving at an assessment of relevant features of that future. The circumstance that this assessment occurs against the background of the realization that this future that one is assessing is, after all, an unknown future is at the heart of what stimulates shrewd entrepreneurial assessments. In peering into the future one is aware that *nothing* is known with certainty about it, not the parameters of any probability functions, or potential surprise functions or anything else.

From this perspective a profit component that emerges from a "lucky" entrepreneurial decision—in the sense that it would be wholly unreasonable to believe the decision maker seriously entertained any expectation that this particular profit component might emerge—is not at all to be dismissed as having played no incentive role. While this particular result was certainly wholly "unexpected" (in Shackle's sense, particularly), it is precisely the entrepreneur's awareness of the potential that the situation held for the wholly unexpected that may have stimulated action and discovery.

To announce in advance to potential entrepreneurs that "lucky" profits will be taxed away is to convert open-ended situations into situations more and more approximating those of a given, closed character. The complete taxing away of pure entrepreneurial profit can, it is clear, succeed only in removing from potential entrepreneurs all incentive for paying attention to anything but the already known (with the "already known" to be interpreted as including what is known concerning the possibilities for costly, deliberate search in the context of a given stochastic environment).

The Taxation of Entrepreneurial Discovery: Remarks on Moral Aspects

The taxation of pure profits, we saw earlier, involves none of the disincentives ("of the first kind") usually discussed in the economic theory of taxation. Without the insights argued in this paper concerning the "second kind" of disincentive that may be associated with the taxation of pure profit, therefore, there appears to be no purely economic reason whatever not to tax away pure profit. (It should be remembered that pure profit is calculated, for our purposes, after deducting from gross revenues an amount sufficient, prospectively, to counterbalance the related risk of economic loss.) Now this conclusion, that the taxation of pure profit entails no undesirable allocative consequences—a conclusion this paper wishes to deny—turns out to reinforce a widely held view of the morality of profit. In this section I take note of this circumstance. I will, further, show that the insights of this paper (pointing out the economic disincentives involved in the taxation of pure profit) permit us to draw attention to moral aspects of pure profits that are not widely appreciated. Thus the questions raised in this paper about the economic desirability of the taxation of profit weaken, at the same time, the moral grounds for considering such taxation wholly justified.

Economic profit has, in the popular judgment, frequently been held to be morally inferior to wage remuneration. This moral inferiority attached to profit appears to be derived from its *surplus* character: profit is a receipt over and above the portion of output needed to ensure the maintenance of existing productive potential. From this perspective many critics of the capitalist system (and perhaps some of its defenders as well) have seen the theories advanced by economists to account for economic profit as somehow seeking to redeem the moral questionableness of profit. The late Joan Robinson put this point of view most bluntly by asserting that the "unconscious preoccupation behind the neo-classical system was chiefly to raise profits to the same level of moral respectability as wages. The labourer is worthy of his hire. What is the capitalist worthy of?"[10]

Now whatever the moral justification economic theory may provide for the share of profit received by the *capitalist*, it should be noticed that such justification does not yet extend to the category of pure entrepreneurial profit. By definition such profit consists of the surplus after the returns to *all* necessary factors of production, including interest on invested capital, have been set aside. No penny of pure entrepreneurial profit can be justified as *needed* to ensure the availability of any necessary productive service. Nor, by the same token, can any penny of pure profit be justified as being the *reward* of any necessary productive effort.

It may be observed that this apparent lack of moral justification for pure profit parallels with precision my discussion of how the category of pure profit possesses no incentive character (of the "first kind") whatever. Everything that is being done in the course of the profitable productive activity would be done even without one penny of profit. The circumstance that removes any incentive character (of the first kind) from pure profit is the same circumstance that, in the popular view, seems to render it morally unjustified. Thus economic reasoning arguing for the economic innocuity of profit taxation is closely related to the reasoning that upholds the moral justification of such taxation.

The reasoning in this paper concerning the disincentive effects of profit taxation impinges on these considerations with obvious significance. On the one hand, my reasoning supports, of course, the insight that pure profit fulfills no incentive role of the first kind. But more important, we have seen that an altogether different incentive role (that of the second kind) is fulfilled by pure profit. Understanding this incentive role for entrepreneurial discovery that is fulfilled by pure profits does not of itself invalidate the reasoning I have cited questioning the moral justifiability of pure profit. After all, it still remains the case that no penny of pure profit was *necessary* to be paid to make it worthwhile for the owner of a productive service to put that service to work for this profitable undertaking; no penny of profit represents the *reward* for productive effort.

Nonetheless our emphasis upon the second kind of incentive role played by pure profit does have several possible moral implications. (1) Pure profit is indeed not necessary, in the narrow meaning of the word, to ensure availability of relevant productive services, *given widespread awareness of the worthwhileness of this productive undertaking*. But it may yet be, as we have seen, that the incentive role of pure profit was a crucial factor in attracting the attention of the successful entrepreneur. It could well be that without such pure profit this productive undertaking would *not*, after all, have been undertaken. (2) Pure profit is indeed not received *in exchange for* any necessary productive service rendered. It is captured by entrepreneurs who were inspired to undertake courses of action whose profitability was "unexpected" by the market at large. This circumstance permits us to recognize profits as having been "created" or, at least, "found" by the insightful entrepreneur. In this way it may be possible to defend the moral justifiability of pure profit by what has been called the "finders-keepers" ethic.[11]

Thus the questions this paper asks concerning the economic desirability of the taxation of pure profit do tend to dovetail, in a clearly specified sense, with the related questions concerning the moral justifiability of such taxation.

The Economics of Taxation: The Scope for Research

In this paper I have critically questioned the unstated premise of the standard theory of taxation. My criticism has rested on our insights into what I have described as incentives of the second kind. But to offer these questions and state these insights is not yet to formulate an economic theory of taxation (or even of the taxation of pure profit); far less is it to develop theoretically sound and administratively practical tax policy. A number of difficult theoretical and practical problems block the way to these goals, at least for the time being. My listing of some of these problems may be organized under two main headings: (a) problems arising out of our ignorance concerning the precise disincentive impacts of different patterns of profit taxation; (b) problems arising out of the practical and empirical difficulties of identifying the pure profit components that are part of more conventional accounting categories, and hence the difficulties in identifying which taxes may in fact involve disincentive effects (of the second kind).

UNSETTLED ISSUES RELATED TO THE DISINCENTIVE IMPACT OF PROFIT TAXATION

I have pursued the insight that the pure profit inherent in economic opportunities may play an incentive role in inspiring the entrepreneurial discovery of those opportunities. This suggested strongly that the taxation of pure profits involves a disincentive not discussed in the standard literature on the economics of taxation. I linked this kind of disincentive to the circumstance that taxing away pure profit tends to convert an "open-ended" situation (which inspires entrepreneurial alertness) into the closed situation in which the alert, wide-awake, resourceful entrepreneur reverts to being the merely routinely consistent, optimizing decision maker within the given, perceived constraints. What is left unclear after these insights are acknowledged is the extent to which the *partial* taxation of profits affects the incentives for discovery. On the one hand it might appear that if profits provide incentive, then *any* reduction in the profit received must be presumed to weaken the incentives for discovery. On the other hand, however, it might be argued that a given percentage tax on prospective pure profit does not significantly erode the *open-endedness* of the situation. It is not, it may be held, the *absolute* levels of pure profit that confer the *open-ended* character upon the entrepreneurial situation. Thus at least moderate taxation of profit may perhaps only slightly affect its incentive power.

Research into the extent of disincentive exercised by this kind of partial taxation of profit might consider the example of the entrepreneurial *partnership.* In such a partnership, too, each entrepreneurial partner can expect only a portion of the pure profits that the partnership may win through his own alertness. To what extent, one wonders, is the individual entrepreneur likely to be better motivated, more likely to perceive opportunities for pure gain, than the entrepreneur who is aware that whatever his own entrepreneurial insight perceives must be shared with a partner, or with the government?

Again, although I have emphasized the importance of pure profits as providing incentives of the second kind, we possess little knowledge of the different degrees in which these incentives might operate in different contexts. The circumstance of "open-endedness" may perhaps operate quite differently in different concrete situations. It appears that such differences in context can be distinguished along several dimensions.

It is well known that entrepreneurial endeavor (and thus pure entrepreneurial profit) may find scope at three distinct levels:[12] (a) the level of pure arbitrage, where paired buying and selling transactions are simultaneous (so that what the successful arbitrageur must "see" is entirely in the virtual present); (b) the level of pure speculation, where simultaneity is absent, so that entrepreneurial alertness must assess the future (but where what is to be sold is physically identical with what was bought); (c) the level of productive *creativity*, where not only is simultaneity absent, but the entrepreneur must also, so to speak, "be alert to" the possibility of combining given inputs into novel forms of product or of obtaining given forms of product from novel combinations of input. At each of these levels the incentive for the entrepreneur to "see" correctly is to be attributed to the open-endedness of the environment. But to see a *present* price differential may call for human qualities different from those that make for shrewd speculation regarding the future. And the qualities of mind and character that stimulate "alert" creativity in production may be altogether different from those that inspire shrewd speculative vision into the future. Research into the sources of entrepreneurial alertness, and into the incentive effects of pure profit, must presumably treat each of these different kinds of entrepreneurial visions separately.

Or again, in modern capitalism a good deal of entrepreneurial vision is exercised *within* complex organizations. In the large modern corporation, for example, there may be many levels at which alert corporate executives may enjoy sufficient discretionary scope, and be stimulated by sufficiently significant opportunities for pure gain for themselves, to require us to recognize these possibilities as representing important examples of entrepreneurial activity. There is every reason, however, to believe that the personal qualities undergirding successful entrepreneurship *within* the modern corporation may fail to overlap entirely with those qualities making for successful entrepreneurship in more conventional contexts. The effect of the taxation of the "pure profit" component in corporate executive rewards may turn out to be significantly different from the effect of taxation on other kinds of entrepreneurial profit. (One possibility for relevant research is suggested by the insights contained in Professor Henry Manne's thesis that legal prohibitions on "insider trading" operate to block the incentives to entrepreneurial discovery on the part of corporate executives).[13]

THE IDENTIFICATION OF PURE PROFIT

The second main heading under which I organize my listing of urgent research needs in the area of entrepreneurial incentives is the empirical identification of pure profits. For policy purposes, any propositions concerning the disincentive effects of the taxation of pure profits must be translated into corresponding statements referring to measurable accounting categories. But we have already seen that accounting profits are both wider and narrower than the category of pure entrepreneurial profit to which my discussions concerning the "second kind" of incentives have pertained. Accounting profits are wider than the category of pure profits, since the former may include implicit interest on invested capital and other nonentrepreneurial categories. Accounting profits are narrower than the category of pure profits insofar as the latter may include elements of entrepreneurial receipts won by the owners of resources, including labor. All this means that the empirical identification of the profit base with respect to which policy pronouncements are to be made calls for careful and insightful research. Professor Shackle was concerned, we saw, with the practical problem of measuring the portion of pure profit attributable to entrepreneurial imagination (as distinct from that attributable to sheer luck). For me, as I noted earlier, Shackle's problem need not perhaps appear to hold significant relevance for practical tax policy. But as we see, measurement difficulties are likely to be severe even if no attempt is made to separate out elements (within the overall category of pure profit) attributable to sheer luck.

But the measurement problem touches on deeper theoretical issues as well as policy issues. The category of pure profit is, after all, one that is linked essentially to *decisions*. Accounting categories, on the other hand, are linked specifically to *periods of time*. Where a long-run decision has been a profitable one (for example, a shrewd decision to build a plant capable of producing what later turns out to be a product in high demand), the entrepreneur may reap immediate accounting profit (as where he sells the plant to eager manufacturers when the strong demand has become apparent to all). But the entrepreneur's profitable decision may not be translated into accounting profits until later periods (as when the entrepreneur operates the plant himself, in a market for which the profitability of this line of production has not yet become widely apparent). Within any given accounting period, therefore, the bare amount of accounting profit recorded reveals little definitive concerning the timing and the nature of the entrepreneurial decisions inspired by these profits.

The problems listed in this section certainly do not exhaust the research agenda that my position seems to call for, if meaningful tax policy is to take account of these concerns. Nor, again, does my position in this paper itself hold promise of any straightforward solutions to these problems. Nonetheless the questions raised, with respect to orthodox tax theory, do appear to demand the attention of theorists and policy analysts. It is for this reason that, inconclusive as my explorations have been, it seems necessary to offer them for consideration.

SIX

The Perils of Regulation: A Market-Process Approach

Introduction

Economists have for at least two centuries debated the merits of government regulation of the market economy. In recent decades, however, this debate appeared to die down, and for a number of years it seemed that economists, with very few exceptions, subscribed to (and indeed helped propagate) a strongly approving view of extensive government intervention in the marketplace. Only recently has the pendulum of professional opinion begun to swing away from a definitely interventionist position, permitting a renewal of the classic debate about government regulation of the economy.

The position in favor of extensive government regulation of the market, of course, must be sharply distinguished from the views of radical critics of capitalism. The interventionist position, unlike that of radical critics, in general thoroughly appreciates the role of the market system in the efficient allocation of resources. The interventionist position fully accepts the central theorem of welfare economics concerning the Pareto optimality achieved, on appropriate assumptions, by the competitive market in general equilibrium. Intervention, however, is said to be required by the real-world impossibility of fulfilling the assumptions needed to hold for a perfectly competitive equilibrium to prevail. Because of chronic "market failure" attributable to the violation of these assumptions, the interventionist position deems it essen-

Reprinted with the permission of the Law and Economics Center, University of Miami, Coral Gables, Florida.

tial that government actively modify the operation of the free market by extensive, even massive, doses of intervention and regulation. The interventionist position holds that the market economy, suitably modified by a judicious combination of government controls on prices, quality of outputs, and the organization of industry, can achieve reasonably satisfactory results. This position came to be so entrenched in professional opinion that, supported (as it always has been) by the layman's intuition, interventionism became a virtually unchallenged orthodoxy.

Only recently has this orthodoxy begun to crumble. Both the layman and the economist have come to suspect that government interventions, especially those limiting competition and controlling prices, are consistently responsible for undesirable consequences. Confidence in the ability of government officials to construct a useful program of controls that would correct "market failure" without generating new problems attributable to government action itself has been rather thoroughly shaken. For many members of the public, and even for many economists, the crumbling of orthodoxy has come as a sharp surprise, if not a jarring shock. Economists now must rethink the theory of the market. They have begun to see that the assumption that the market can approximate a competitive equilibrium is more robust than hitherto believed. They have argued that government regulation produces its own undesirable distortions in market outcomes. Finally, economists have begun to understand that the political economy of regulation tends to ensure that market interventions are far more likely to be undertaken to further the well-being of special interests (not excepting those of the regulators themselves) than of the public at large.

This essay, too, draws attention to problems that appear to be the inescapable results of government regulation of the market. However, the approach taken here differs substantially from those just mentioned in that it does not postulate instantaneous or even rapid achievement of a general equilibrium in the free market; nor does it emphasize the undesirable distortions in equilibrium conditions introduced by government regulation. And to simplify matters, the discussion will relate to controls assumed to be deliberately introduced and enforced by legislators and officials intent on nothing but the welfare of the consuming public. The position developed here argues that intervention tends to interfere harmfully in the *entrepreneurial process* upon which the most basic of the market's virtues (conceded in principle by its interventionist critics) must surely depend.

To avoid misunderstanding, it should be emphasized that I do not wish to minimize the impact of those implications of regulation upon which my own argument does *not* rest. There can be little doubt that much regulation has been inspired, consciously or not, by considerations other than the goal of contributing to the public weal.[1] And the propensity of government interventions to generate tendencies toward suboptimal equilibrium configurations has certainly been amply demonstrated by economists from Bastiat to Friedman.[2] I merely contend that, valid though these approaches to a critique of interventionism undoubtedly are, they do not exhaust the phenomena to be explained. To sharpen the presentation of the approach taken here, regulations are assumed to be introduced and enforced with only the public welfare in mind. Many of regulation's undesirable consequences undoubtedly can be attributed to the tendency for regulation to serve the interests of regulators. I maintain that, quite apart from such difficulties, regulation generates economic confusion and inefficiency. This confusion and inefficiency are perceived more clearly by assuming, for the sake of argument, that those *other* difficulties (arising out of the regulators' self-interest) are absent.

Interventionism and Socialism: A Parallel

The surprise and dismay experienced today by so many economists and others at the manifest failure of

well-meaning interventionist measures to create anything but inefficiencies of their very own is reminiscent
in many ways of the surprise and disquiet experienced
some sixty years ago when Mises first demonstrated on
theoretical grounds, the inability of a socialized economy
to perform the economic calculation needed for social efficiency. It is instructive to pursue this parallel further,
for properly understood, Mises's theoretical argument regarding the socialist (that is, nonmarket) economy suggests useful insights into the problems of the hampered
(that is, regulated) market economy. It was the earlier
failure (by Mises's readers) to understand the operation
and function of the market economy that led them to assume uncritically that a socialist society, in principle,
need encounter no difficulty in the attainment of social
efficiency. The realization that this assumption was far
from obviously justified occasioned the surprise and disquiet following Mises's famous article. The now crumbling orthodoxy upon which the interventionist approach
until very recently has rested reflects misunderstandings
concerning the operation and function of markets. And
those misunderstandings bear a remarkable likeness to
those pointed out by Mises, and later by Hayek. These
deep-rooted misunderstandings, in turn, appear responsible for the surprise and dismay occasioned by the realization that government regulation may itself be the problem rather than the solution it had so obviously seemed
to be.

The hampered, regulated market, of course, is not at
all the same thing as the fully socialized economy which
Mises and Hayek studied. In the socialized economy
there is no market at all, free or otherwise, for the services
of material factors. In the socialized economy, therefore,
there can be no market prices for such factor services.
This absence of market prices is crucial to the Mises-Hayek critique of socialism. The regulated market economy,
on the other hand, no matter how hampered it may be, *is*
unquestionably a market economy, in which prices

emerge through the interplay of profit-seeking market transactions. The Mises-Hayek critique of socialism, therefore, is certainly not applicable, as it stands, to the regulated market.

A brief review of the Mises-Hayek critique of socialism nonetheless proves helpful for a critical appraisal of regulation. For the Mises-Hayek discussion offers an appreciation for the operation of the market process by revealing the enormous difficulties confronting socialist planners trying to emulate the market economy's achievements without a market. This discussion also reveals the hazards besetting the path of regulators seeking to improve on the market's performance. Just as the attempt to seek social efficiency through central planning rather than through the spontaneous market process, in the Mises-Hayek view, must necessarily fail, so too, for essentially similar reasons, must attempts to control the outcomes of the spontaneous market by deliberate, extra-market, regulatory action necessarily tend to generate unexpected and wholly undesired consequences.

I turn, therefore, to a brief review of the debate on socialist economic calculation, drawing particular attention to a widespread failure to appreciate fully certain important elements in the Mises-Hayek critique. It is these important elements, indeed, that will be found to be the basis for this essay's critical analysis of government regulation of the market economy. These elements underlie our perception of the parallel between a critique of the regulated market on the one hand and of socialism, without any market at all, on the other.

MISES AND HAYEK ON SOCIALISM

Mises's demonstration of the economic calculation problem facing the socialist planning authorites was first presented in 1920.[3] The demonstration was subsequently repeated in more or less similar terms (with critical attention paid to the attempts of socialist writers to respond to his challenge) in several of Mises's later works.[4] Hayek first addressed the problem in two essays, which respectively introduced and summed up the debate concerning socialist calculation (in the volume of essays on the subject that he edited in 1935).[5] An important third essay, published in 1940, contains Hayek's most complete appraisal of the issues.[6] Many writers on the Continent, in England, and in the United States attempted to meet Mises's arguments, the best-known socialist contribution being that of Oskar Lange.[7] A thorough survey of the state of literature at the onset of World War II, provided by a Norwegian economist, was made available in English in 1949.[8]

For Mises, the defining element in socialism lies in its collective ownership of the means of production, in particular land and capital. It follows, therefore, that under socialism there exists no market for these factors of production or for their services; without private ownership, there can be no market exchanges between individual owners; and without market exchanges, of course, there can be no ratios of exchange—that is, there can be no market prices. Mises finds in the absence of factor prices the essence of the difficulty. Without prices, socialist decision makers (the central planners and their subordinates, the managers of socialized enterprises) do not have available relevant indicators (prices) of the relative economic importance of the various factor services in their various alternative uses. Socialist planners cannot know whether the allocation of a unit of a particular resource to a specific line of production is more or less desirable than its replacement by some quantity of another resource which is technologically capable of substituting for the first. Planners cannot know in advance where efficiency is likely to be attained, nor do they have any way of assessing ex post whether or to what extent such efficiency may have been achieved.

Professor Armentano illustrates Mises's point by imagining a socialist director choosing between the construction of a power plant that uses fossil fuel and one that uses nuclear fuel. Since the state owns all of the resources, no objective money prices exist for any of the alternative projects' required resources. The socialist planner has no way of knowing which project is cheaper, which promises the greater return on investment, which, in sum, offers the most efficient way to produce electricity. "If and when the power plant is built at a particular point with particular resources, it will represent an 'arbitrary' and not an economic decision."[9]

Hayek's most complete discussion of the problem of socialist calculation appeared in 1940 as a review article analyzing particularly the contributions of two socialist economists, Oskar Lange and H. D. Dickinson.[10] Both Lange and Dickinson conceded that economic calculation is unthinkable without factor prices.[11] They pointed out, however, that a price need not mean merely an exchange ratio established in a market; the notion of price, they maintained, can be understood more broadly as "the terms on which alternatives are offered." Using price in this broader sense, they argued, there is every possibility for setting up a socialist economy in which "prices" are announced by the planning authorities and are used as guides in the decisions of socialist managers (who are instructed to obey specified rules in which these "prices" appear). These writers believed the authorities could handle the adjustment of prices on the basis of trial and error, with the relation between perceived supply and demand indicating to the authorities where adjustments should be made. In this fashion, the socialist writers held, a socialist economy could achieve an efficient allocation of resources without markets in the material factors of production, and without profit-maximizing entrepreneurial decisions.

Hayek's critique of the Lange-Dickinson proposals was long and detailed. He considered their approach to be a vast improvement as compared with the earlier socialist reactions to Mises, in which the nature of the problem was hardly perceived at all. Yet he continued to find the

Lange-Dickinson proposals seriously deficient both in their perception of the problem to be solved and of the practical difficulties confronting the suggested solution. The difference, Hayek wrote, between the "system of regimented prices" proposed by the socialist economists "and a system of prices determined by the market seems to be about the same as that between an attacking army in which every unit and every man could move only by special command and by the exact distance ordered by headquarters and an army in which every unit and every man can take advantage of every opportunity offered to them."[12]

Some Thoughts on the Socialist Calculation Literature

Despite Hayek's powerful critique of the Lange-Dickinson proposals, the postwar textbook literature, curiously, came to present the results of the interwar debate as if Mises's original claim (to have demonstrated the impossiblity of economic calculation under socialism) had been decisively refuted by Lange, Dickinson, and Lerner.[13] Several writers have noted that this view conveyed by the literature is seriously mistaken.[14] A careful review of the debate surely reveals that the Lange-Dickinson-Lerner solution hardly comes to grips with the difficulties that Mises and Hayek explained. The textbook literature did not so much ignore the arguments of Mises and Hayek *as it failed to understand the view of the market process, which underlies their critique of socialist calculation.* Indeed, the authors of the socialist proposals themselves offered their solution from a perspective on the nature and function of the market economy that differed sharply from the "Austrian" perspective shared by Mises and Hayek. My purpose in drawing attention to this defective view of the market reflected in the Lange-Dickinson literature is not merely to throw light on the socialist calculation debate (an issue only tangentially relevant to our own theme of efficiency in the regulated market economy); for the insights into the market process expressed in the Mises-Hayek view and overlooked in the Lange-Dickinson proposal become crucial to a critique of the economics of regulation.

Lange's response to Mises placed much emphasis on the *"parametric function of prices,* i.e., on the fact that . . . each individual separately regards the actual market prices as given data to which he has to adjust himself."[15] For Lange, each person in the market treats prices as if they were equilibrium prices to which he must adjust himself passively. If the market prices happen *not* to be equilibrium prices, then these market prices must somehow change "by a series of successive trials"— prices rising where demand exceeds supply, and so on.[16] Lange does not address the question of *how* market prices actually change if each person at all times considers prices as given data to which he must silently adjust himself.

For Lange, indeed, the function that prices play in the efficiency of markets is simply the function that the equilibrium set of prices would fill. Prices, that is, provide the parameters to guide market participants in engaging in the set of activities that are consistent with equilibrium conditions. Lange understandably held that this function of prices could be simulated in a socialist economy. Socialist managers can be given lists of "prices" to which they can react according to well-defined rules (analogous to, but of course not identical with, the "rule" that capitalist decision makers are assumed to follow: that is, to maximize profits), Lange believed the task of ensuring that the lists of "prices" would be those required to ensure overall efficiency in the socialist economy could be fulfilled by again simulating (what he thought to be) the market trial and error procedure.

But here lies Lange's cardinal misunderstanding: he assumed that there exists in the market a procedure (involving "a series of successive trials") whereby prices are somehow adjusted toward equilibrium *without essen-*

*tially altering the "parametric" character and function
of prices* (that is, without departing from the supposition
that each person separately regards market prices as given
data, which he is unable to change). The market process
through which prices are adjusted toward equilibrium,
however, is a process in which prices are *not* treated as
given parameters but are themselves hammered out in
the course of vigorous and rivalrous bidding.

In emphasizing exclusively the "parametric" function of market prices. Lange misunderstood the central
role of the market. The primary function of the market is
not to offer an arena within which market participants
can have their decentralized decisions smoothly coordinated through attention to the appropriate list of given
prices. The market's essential function, rather, is to offer
an arena in which market participants, by entrepreneurial
exploitation of the profit opportunities offered by disequilibrium prices, can nudge prices in the direction of equilibrium. In this entrepreneurial process prices are *not*
treated as parameters. Nor, in this process, are prices
changed impersonally in response to excess demand or
supply. It is one thing for Lange to assume that socialist
managers can be motived to follow rules with respect to
centrally promulgated given "prices" (in the way capitalist decision makers can be imagined to treat given
equilibrium market prices).[17] It is quite another to assume that the *non*-parametric function of price in the
market system, the function dependent on entrepreneurial alertness to opportunities for pure profit, can be
simulated in a system from which the entrepreneurial
function has been wholly excised.

That Lange did not understand this nonparametric
function of prices must certainly be attributed to a perception of the market system's operation primarily in
terms of perfectly competitive equilibrium. (Indeed, it is
this textbook approach to price theory that Lange explicitly presents as his model for socialist pricing.[18])
Within this paradigm, as is now well recognized, the role

of the entrepreneurial quest for pure profit, as the key element in bringing about price adjustment, is completely ignored. It is not difficult to see how Lange could conclude that such a (nonentrepreneurial) system might be simulated under socialism.

Mises and Hayek, by contrast, saw the price system under capitalism from a totally different—an Austrian—perspective. For these writers, the essence of the market process lies not in the "parametric" function of price, and not in the perfectly competitive state of equilibrium, but in the rivalrous activity of entrepreneurs taking advantage of disequilibrium conditions. The debate between Lange-Dickinson on the one hand and Mises-Hayek on the other can best be understood as a clash between two conflicting views of the price system. Mises's views on the market as a process have been expounded extensively in a number of his works.[19] The idea of the market as a *dynamic process* is at the very heart of his system. Hayek's perception of the price system was articulated (during the same period in which his critical essays on socialist calculation were written) in a remarkable series of papers on the role of knowledge and discovery in market processes.[20]

That the postwar textbooks incorrectly presented the debate on socialist calculation as having been decisively won by Lange must be attributed not to ideological bias (although this may not have been entirely absent) but to an utter failure to understand the flaws in Lange's discussion (flaws that Hayek indeed had identified). Not recognizing the Austrian background of Hayek's critique, Anglo-American economists saw in Lange a cogent application of standard price theory; Hayek's critique simply was not understood.

THE MARKET PROCESS: AN AUSTRIAN VIEW[21]

Before returning to the theme of efficiency in the regulated economy, it is useful to review some Austrian lessons to be drawn from the socialist calculation debate.

The Austrian understanding of the market as a dynamic process of discovery generated by the entrepreneurial-competitive scramble for pure profit may be spelled out in terms of a brief discussion of several key concepts. A sensitive appreciation of these ideas will alert us to problems raised by government regulation of the market that might otherwise easily be overlooked. It is partly because the terms convenient for the exposition of these concepts also are used in non-Austrian contexts, with rather different meanings, that the ideas developed here are so often misunderstood and therefore require brief elaboration.

Competition. What keeps the market process in motion is competition—*not* competition in the sense of "perfect competition," in which perfect knowledge is combined with very large numbers of buyers and sellers to generate a state of perennial equilibrium—but competition as the rivalrous activities of market participants trying to win profits by offering the market better opportunities than are currently available. The existence of rivalrous competition requires *not* large numbers of buyers and sellers but simply *freedom of entry.* Competition places pressure on market participants to discover where and how better opportunities, as yet unnoticed, *might* be offered to the market. The competitive market process occurs because equilibrium has not yet been attained. This process is thwarted whenever nonmarket barriers are imposed blocking entry to potential competitors.

Knowledge and Discovery. As Hayek has emphasized, the competitive market process is a discovery procedure.[22] If all that needed to be known were already known, then the market would already have attained full equilibrium, the state in which all decisions correctly anticipate all other decisions being made within the market. An institutional device for social organization that mobilizes existing knowledge and brings it to bear upon decision makers is necessary because realistically people never do have command even over all the information that is already known somewhere.[23] Market equilibrium is thinkable only if we can presuppose the full mobilization of existing knowledge; so also centralized economic control would be thinkable (whether by Lange-Dickinson-Lerner proposals or other devices) if we could assume existing knowledge already to be fully mobilized. It is just because, without a market, such prior mobilization is so difficult to assume that a market is seen to be a prerequisite for economic calculation.

The competitive market process is needed not only to mobilize existing knowledge, but also to generate awareness of opportunities whose very existence until now has been known to no one at all.[24] The entrepreneurial process, moreover, disseminates existing information through the market. The process itself is a continual one of the discovery of opportunities. The discoverer of these opportunities himself, at least, has had no inkling whatever of their very existence. The market, in other words, is not merely a process of search for information of the need for which men had previously been aware; it is a discovery procedure that tends to correct ignorance where the discoverers themselves were totally unaware that they indeed were ignorant. A realization that the market yields knowledge—the sort of knowledge that people do not at present even know they need—should engender among would-be social engineers who seek to replace or to modify the results of the free market a very definite sense of humility. To announce that one can improve on the performance of the market, one must also claim to know in advance what the market will reveal. This knowledge is clearly impossible in all circumstances. Indeed, where the market process has been thwarted, in general it will not be possible to point with certainty to what *might* have been discovered that has now been lost.

Profit and Incentives. In standard treatments of price theory, decision makers are assumed to maximize utility or "profit." The profit for which entrepreneurs are so eager (and which for Austrians drives the market process) is *not* that "profit" maximized by the firm in the standard theory of the firm. The standard theory assumes that the firm confronts definitely known and given cost and revenue possibilities. For the theory of the firm, therefore, to maximize profits does not mean *to discover* an opportunity for pure gain; it means merely to perform the mathematical calculations required to exhaust the *already fully perceived* opportunity for gain that the given revenue and cost curves might present. The urge of would-be entrepreneurs to grasp profit, by contrast, is the force which *itself reveals* the existence of gaps between costs and revenues. This distinction is of considerable importance.

It is elementary to the theory of the market that the market performs its functions by virtue of the *incentives* it offers to those who make "correct" decisions. For example, the incentive of the higher wages offered by industries in which the marginal productivity of labor is greatest attracts labor to more important uses. Such incentives tend to ensure that once a superior use for a given factor (or group of factors) is discovered, it becomes worthwhile for factor owners to forgo alternative ways of putting their factors to work. This is well understood. What is not always understood is that the market also offers incentives for the *discovery* of new opportunities (for the most useful employment of factors), that is, for the exploitation of opportunities that until now have remained unexploited. These opportunities have remained unexploited *not* because of high costs, and not even because of the high cost of searching for them. They have remained unexploited simply because of sheer oversight, possibly including oversight of the opportunity to find them through deliberate search. Pure entrepreneurial profit is the market form in which *this* kind of incentive presents itself. The availability of pure entrepreneurial profit has the function not of outweighing the costs associated with withdrawing inputs from alternative uses, but of alerting decision makers to the present error of committing factors to uses less valuable to the markets than others waiting and able to be served.

Market Prices. Market prices in the Austrian view are not primarily approximations to the set of equilibrium prices. Instead, they are (disequilibrium) exchange ratios worked out between entrepreneurial market participants. On the one hand, these exchange ratios with all their imperfections reflect the discoveries made up until this moment by profit-seeking entrepreneurs. On the other hand, these ratios express entrepreneurial errors currently being made. Market prices, therefore, offer opportunities for pure profit. And we can rely on these opportunities to create a tendency for market prices to be changed through the rivalrous bidding of alert entrepreneurs. The course of market prices, in other words, is closely bound up, in *two* distinct ways, with the incentive system of pure entrepreneurial profit. First, the configuration of market prices at any given moment must be attributed to the pure profit incentives that have until now determined bids and offers. Second, this present configuration of market prices, together with existing and future conditions of supply and demand, is responsible for the opportunities for pure profit. The discovery and exploitation of these opportunities will constitute the course of the market process in the immediate future. From this perspective on market prices it is not difficult to perceive how small must be the resemblance to them of any centrally promulgated set of socialist "prices." The entrepreneurial drive for pure profit plays no role at all in the determination of socialist "prices."

Regulated Market Economy

I shall assume, as noted at the outset of this essay, that government regulation of the market economy is

generated by dissatisfaction with market outcomes. Legislators or other government officials (perhaps in response
to public outcry, or in anticipation thereof) are disturbed
either by the high price that certain would-be purchasers
are asked to pay in the market or by the low price (for
example, farm prices or the wages of labor) received by
certain sellers in the market; or they are disturbed by the
quality of goods or services being offered for sale (for example, because of the absence of safety devices) or by the
unavailability in the market of goods or services that they
believe to be important. They are disturbed by the conditions under which workers are expected to work, or they
are disturbed by the pattern of income distribution generated by the market, by unemployment, or by "profiteer-
ing," or by the side effects (such as environmental pollu-
tion, or spread of disease, or exposure of the young to pornography) generated by uncontrolled market activity.

Hoping to correct what are perceived to be unsatisfactory conditions, the government intervenes in the
market. It seeks to replace the outcomes expected to result from unchecked market transactions by a preferred
configuration of prices and outputs, to be achieved not, as
under socialism, by replacing the market by central
ownership of factors, but by imposing appropriate regulations and controls. The laissez-faire market is replaced by
the regulated market. Price ceilings and price and wage
floors, transfers of incomes, imposed safety standards,
child labor laws, zoning laws, prohibited industrial integration, tariff protection, prohibited competition, imposed health warnings, compulsory old age pensions, and
prohibited drugs are all examples of the countless controls that well-meaning public officials impose.

In the face of these controls, regulations, and interventions there remains, nonetheless, a genuine market
both for factor services and for consumer products. Government controls constrain and constrict; they rearrange
and repattern the structure of incentives; they redistrib-

ute incomes and wealth and sharply modify both the processes of production and the composition of consumption. Yet within the limits that such controls impose, buying and selling continue, and the constant effort to capture pure entrepreneurial gain keeps the market in perpetual motion. Government regulations drastically alter and disturb opportunities for entrepreneurial gain, but they do not eliminate them. These controls thoroughly influence the prices that emerge from the interplay of entrepreneurial competition. But unless directly mandated prices are involved, exchange ratios still reflect the outcome to date of the entrepreneurial process.

Traditionally, criticism of government intervention involves one of more of several general lines of argument.[25] First, critics may argue that the admitted failure of market outcomes to meet successfully the aspirations of regulators is a result not of market failure to achieve peak efficiency, but of inescapable scarcity. If costs are fully taken into account, efforts to improve outcomes must be found to be doomed to failure or to lead to even less preferable outcomes. Second, critics may agree that from the viewpoint of the value system adopted by the would-be regulators market outcomes might be improved upon. But, these critics maintain that the market faithfully reflects consumers' values. Regulation in such circumstances therefore must violate consumer sovereignty, if not consumer freedom.

Third, critics may argue that the unwished-for market outcomes are to be attributed not to the free market, but to earlier government interventions in the market which have hindered the corrective forces of the market from doing their work. Additional regulation, it is then pointed out, either may be unnecessary (since the earlier interventions can simply be eliminated) or may compound the problems. Fourth, critics may argue that whether or not the undesirable outcomes of the market are (in the sense appropriate to economic science and not necessarily from the viewpoint of the regulators' values) to be regretted, government regulation is simply incapable of achieving improvement. The technology of regulation is such that its full costs outweigh by far any benefits that may be achieved.

The Austrian lessons drawn from the preceding survey of the debate about socialist economic calculation suggest that another set of considerations, until now not sufficiently emphasized in the literature, deserve to be included in the list of causes to which one might attribute the failures of regulation. These considerations constitute a separate line of critcism of government intervention, to be added to the other lines of criticism (where one or more of these may be relevant).[26]

GOVERNMENT REGULATION AND THE MARKET DISCOVERY PROCESS

The perils associated with government regulation of the economy addressed here arise out of the *impact that regulation can be expected to have on the discovery process, which the unregulated market tends to generate.* Even if current market outcomes in some sense are judged unsatisfactory, intervention, and even intervention that can successfully achieve its immediate objectives, cannot be considered the obviously correct solution. After all, the very problems apparent in the market might generate processes of discovery and correction superior to those undertaken deliberately by government regulation; deliberate intervention by the state not only might serve as an imperfect substitute for the spontaneous market process of discovery; but also might impede desirable processes of discovery the need for which has *not* been perceived by the government. Again, government regulation itself may generate new (unintended and undesired) processes of market adjustments that produce a final outcome even less preferred than what might have emerged in the free market.

Here I discuss critically the impact of government regulation on the discovery process of the unregulated market at four distinct levels. First, I consider the likelihood that would-be regulators may not correctly assess the course the market might itself take in the absence of regulation. Second, I consider the likelihood that, because of the presumed absence of entrepreneurial incentives operating on government decision makers, government regulatory decisions will fail to exploit opportunities for social betterment waiting to be discovered. Third, I consider the likelihood that government regulation may stifle or inhibit desirable discovery processes which the market might have generated. Finally, I consider the likelihood that government regulation may influence the market by creating opportunities for new, and not necessarily desirable, market discovery processes which would not be relevant in an unregulated market.

THE UNDISCOVERED DISCOVERY PROCESS

We assumed earlier that regulation is demanded because of undesirable conditions that emerge in the market in the absence of regulation. But the urge to regulate, to control, to alter these outcomes must presume not only that these undesirable conditions are attributable to the absence of regulation, but also that the speedy removal of such conditions cannot be expected from the future course of unregulated market events. To attribute undesirable conditions to absence of regulation, moreover, also may require the denial of the proposition that were a better state of affairs indeed feasible, the market probably would have already discovered how to achieve it.

More specifically, many demands for government intervention into the market rest on one or both of two possible misunderstandings concerning the market discovery process. Demand for government intervention, on the one hand, might grow out of a failure to realize that the market already may have discovered virtually everything worth discovering (so that what appears to be obvious inefficiency might be able to be explained alto-gether satisfactorily if government officials had all the in-formation the market has long since discovered and taken advantage of). Demand for regulation, on the other hand, may stem from the belief that unsatisfactory conditions will never be corrected unless by deliberate intervention. Such demands for regulation might be muted, that is, were it understood that genuine inefficiencies can be re-lied upon in the *future* to generate market processes for their own correction. (This second misunderstanding it-self may rest on either of two bases. First, the tendency of markets to discover and eliminate inefficiency simply is not recognized. Second, by contrast, it is assumed, far too sanguinely, that market processes are *so* rapid that our awareness of an unmistakably unsatisfactory condition proves that some kind of market "failure" has occurred and that one cannot rely on future corrective processes.)

These misunderstandings, so often the foundation for demands for intervention, surely derive from an un-awareness of several basic principles of the theory of mar-ket process. These principles show that, first, were knowledge perfect, it would be inconceivable that unex-ploited opportunities could yet remain for rearranging the pattern of input utilization or output consumption in such a way as to improve the well-being of all market participants; second, the existence of such unexploited opportunities, reflecting imperfect knowledge through-out the market, expresses itself in the unregulated market in the form of opportunities for pure entrepreneurial prof-it; and third, the tendency for such pure profit oppor-tunities to be discovered and exploited tends more or less rapidly to eliminate unexploited opportunities for im-proving the allocation of resources.[27] These principles of the theory of market process suggest that if genuine inef-ficiency exists, then (perhaps because of a recent sudden change in conditions of resource supply, of technology, or of consumer tastes) the market has not yet discovered *all that it will surely soon tend to discover.*

These principles may be denied either by expressing a lack of confidence in the systematic tendency for imperfect knowledge to be spontaneously improved or by attributing to the market the ability to attain equilibrium instantaneously (that is, by assuming that ignorance is not merely a disequilibrium phenomenon, but that ignorance disappears the very instant it emerges). Both denials may lead to demands for government intervention. The denial based on a lack of confidence about improving knowledge leads to the belief that current inefficiencies will not tend to be corrected spontaneously (and also to the propensity to see inefficiency where the market *already* has made necessary corrections). The denial based on the belief in instantaneous correction of disequilibrium conditions leads to the view that existing inefficiencies somehow are consistent with market equilibrium and that therefore extramarket steps are called for to achieve correction.

THE UNSIMULATED DISCOVERY PROCESS

Government regulation takes the general form of imposed price ceilings and floors, of mandated quality specifications, and of other restraints or requirements imposed in interpersonal market transactions. The hope surrounding such government impositions, I continue to assume, is that they will constrain market activities to desired channels and at desired levels. But what is the likelihood that government officials, with the best of intentions, will *know* what imposed prices, say, might evoke the "correct," desired actions by market participants? This question parallels that raised by Mises and Hayek with respect to "market" socialism.[28] Government officials in the regulated economy do enjoy the advantage (*not* shared by socialist planning officials) of making their decisions within the framework of genuine market prices. But the question remains: How do government officials know what prices to set (or qualities to require, and so forth)? Or to press the point further: How will government officials know if their earlier decisions were in error and in what direction to make corrections? In other words, how will government officials *discover* those opportunities for improving the allocation of resources, which one cannot assume to be automatically known to them at the outset of a regulatory endeavor?

The compelling insight underlying these questions rests heavily on the circumstance that officials institutionally are precluded from capturing *pecuniary* profits in the market, in the course of their activities (even though they are as eager as anyone else for entrepreneurial "profit" in the broadest sense of the term). The regulators' estimates of the prices consumers are prepared to pay, or of the prices resource owners are prepared to accept, for example, *are not profit-motivated estimates.* The estimates are not profit motivated at the time of an initial government regulatory action, and they are not profit motivated at each subsequent date when modification of a regulation might be considered. But estimates of market demand conditions or market supply conditions that are not profit motivated cannot reflect the powerful, discovery-inspiring incentives of the entrepreneurial quest for profit.

Nothing in the course of the regulatory process suggests a tendency for as yet unperceived opportunities of resource allocation improvement to be discovered. Nothing ensures that government officials who might perceive market conditions more accurately than others will tend systematically to replace less competent regulators. There is no entrepreneurial process at work, and there is no proxy for entrepreneurial profit or loss that easily might indicate where errors have been made and how they should be corrected. What regulators know (or believe they know) at a given moment presumably remains only partly correct. No systematic process seems at work through which regulators might come to discover what they have not known, *especially since they have not known that they enjoy less than complete awareness of a particular situation.*

The problem raised here is not quite the same as the one identified in other literature critical of government intervention. It is often noted, for example, that government officials are not motivated to minimize costs, since they will not personally benefit from the resulting economies.[29] The problem raised here differs importantly from such questions of incentives for adopting known efficiencies. For even if one could imagine an official so dedicated to the citizenry that he would ensure the adoption of all known possible measures for cutting costs, one cannot yet imagine him somehow divining *as yet undiscovered* techniques for cutting costs. What the offical knows, he knows, and what he knows that he does *not* know, one may imagine him diligently undertaking to find out, through appropriate cost-benefit-calculated search. But one can hardly imagine him discovering, except by the sheerest accident, those opportunities for increasing efficiency of which he is completely unaware. The official is not subject to the entrepreneurial profit incentive, which somehow appears continually and successfully to inspire discovery of hitherto undreamed of possibilities for eliminating unnecessary expenditures. Nothing within the regulatory process seems able to simulate even remotely well the discovery process that is so integral to the unregulated market.

THE STIFLED DISCOVERY PROCESS

The most serious effect of government regulation on the market discovery process well might be the likelihood that regulation, in a variety of ways, may discourage, hamper, and even completely stifle the discovery process of the unregulated market. Indeed, that much regulation is introduced as a result of unawareness of the market's discovery process already has been noted.

Government regulation plainly might bar exploitation of opportunities for pure entrepreneurial profit. A price ceiling, a price floor, an impeded merger, or an imposed safety requirement might block possibly profitable entrepreneurial actions. Such restraints and requirements may be designed to block *particular* activities. If so, the likelihood is that since the possibility of such activities is so clearly seen and feared, the blocked activity may provide standard rates of return, but *not* particularly profitable ones in the entrepreneurial sense. Regulated restraints and requirements, though, are also likely to block activities that have *not* yet been foreseen by anyone, including the regulatory authorities. Regulatory constraints, that is, are likely *to bar the discovery* of pure profit opportunities.

That government regulation diminishes competition is common knowledge. Tariffs, licensing requirements, labor legislation, airline regulation, and bank regulation reduce the number of potential participants in particular markets. Government regulation, therefore, is responsible for imposing monopolylike inefficiencies ("deadweight" welfare losses) upon the economy. But such losses by no means constitute the full impact of the countercompetitive measures often embodied in regulatory constraints.

The beneficent aspect of competition in the sense of a rivalrous process, as noted earlier, arises out of *freedom of entry.* What government regulations so often erect are *regulatory barriers to entry.* Freedom of "entry," for the Austrian approach, refers to the freedom of potential competitors to discover and to move to exploit existing opportunities for pure profit. If entry is blocked, such opportunities simply may never be discovered, either by existing firms in the industry, or by regulatory authorities, or for that matter by outside entrepreneurs who *might* have discovered such opportunities were they allowed to be exploited when found.

From *this* perspective on regulation's anticompetitive impact, it follows that much regulation introduced explicitly to *create* or *maintain* competition is no less hazardous to the competitive-entrepreneurial process than are other forms of regulation that restrict competition. Entry of competitors, in the dynamic sense, need not mean entry of firms of about equal size. For example, entry might imply the *replacement,* by merger or other means, of a number of relatively high-cost producers by a *single* low-cost producer. Antitrust activity designed ostensibly to protect competition might *block* this kind of entry. Such regulatory activity thus blocks the capture of pure profit, obtainable in this case by the discovery and implementation of the possibility of lowering the price to consumers by taking advantage of hitherto unexploited, and perhaps unsuspected, economies of scale.

The literature critical of government regulation often draws attention to the undesirable effects of imposed prices. A price ceiling for a particular product or service (rent control, for example) tends to generate artificial shortages (of housing). A price floor for a particular product or service, (minimum wages, for example) tends to generate an artificial surplus (teenage unemployment). These important, well-recognized consequences of imposed prices flow from the efforts of the regulators to legislate prices at other than equilibrium levels.

Quite apart from the discoordination generated by such imposed prices in the markets for *existing* goods and services, price (and also quality) restraints also may well inhibit the discovery of wholly new opportunities. A price ceiling does not merely block the upper reaches of a given supply curve. Such a ceiling also may inhibit the discovery of as yet unsuspected sources of supply (which in the absence of the ceiling would have tended to shift the entire supply curve to the right) or of as yet wholly unknown new products (tending to create supply curves for wholly new graphs).[30] The lure of pure profit tends to uncover such as yet unknown opportunities.

Price and quality restraints and requirements and restrictions on organizational forms operate (in a generally understood but not precisely predictable way) to inhibit entrepreneurial discovery. Price ceilings, for example, not only restrict supply from known sources of natural gas (or from known prospects for search), but also inhibit the dis-

covery of wholly unknown sources. Drug testing regulations, as another example, not only reduce the flow of
new pharmaceutical drugs where successful research
might have been more or less predictable, but also discourage the entrepreneurial discovery of wholly unknown research procedures. Against whatever benefits
might be derived from government regulation and intervention, one is forced to weigh, as one of regulation's in-
trinsically immeasurable costs, the stifling of the market
discovery process.

THE WHOLLY SUPERFLUOUS DISCOVERY PROCESS

There is yet one more aspect of government regulation's complex impact on the discovery process. Whether
intended by the regulatory authorities or not and whether
suspected by them or not, the imposition of regulatory
restraints and requirements tends to create entirely new,
and not necessarily desirable opportunities for entrepreneurial discovery.

That such opportunities may be created follows
from the extreme unlikelihood that government-imposed
price, quality, or quantity constraints introduce anything
approaching an equilibrium configuration. These constraints, on the contrary, introduce pure profit opportunities that would otherwise have been absent, as they
simultaneously reduce or possibly eliminate other opportunities for pure profit that might otherwise have existed.
This rearrangement of opportunities for pure profits, of
course, is unlikely to be the explicit aim of regulation;
nor even, indeed, is such rearrangement ever likely to be
fully *known* to the authorities. Market ignorance is a fact
of economic life. It follows that the replacement of one
set of (unregulated) prices by another set of (partly regulated) prices, simply means that regulation has generated
a possibly major alteration in the pattern of the discovery
process. The now regulated market will tend to pursue
the altered discovery process.

This regulation-induced alteration in the pattern of
market discovery is closely related to the often noticed

circumstance that regulation may result in a different set of *equilibrium* market consequences. Such consequences, moreover, may not have been correctly foretold by the authorities and, indeed, may be wholly undesired by them. Regulation often imposes costs not immediately recognized.[31] Unless, quite fantastically, the regulatory authorities (somehow all acting in completely coordinated fashion) are perfectly informed on all relevant data about the market, they will *not* generally be able to perceive what new profit opportunities they create by their own regulatory actions. Inevitably, therefore, the imposition of a set of regulatory constraints on a market must set in motion a series of entrepreneurial actions that have *not* been anticipated and, therefore, that may well lead to wholly unexpected and even undesired final outcomes.[32]

The one kind of new "profit" opportunity created by regulation that is by now well anticipated, though hardly desired of course, involves bribery and corruption of the regulators. There is widespread understanding of the unwholesome channels into which the entrepreneurial quest for pure profit inevitably tends to be attracted if arbitrary restraints on otherwise profitable activities are imposed.[33]

The basic insight underlying these conclusions, in sum, is a simple one. The competitive-entrepreneurial process, being a process of discovery of the as yet unknown, can hardly be predicted in any but the broadest terms. The imposition of regulatory constraints necessarily results, therefore, in a pattern of consequences different from and, most plausibly, distinctly less desirable than what would have occurred in the unregulated market. One might therefore refer to this unplanned, undesired pattern of consequences of regulation as the wholly superfluous discovery process.

Discovery, Evidence, and Illustration

The preceding discussion is theoretical and general, providing no hints of possible verification of its conclusions. While this discussion relies on highly plausible insights into the character of human action, a reader may believe himself justified in demanding evidence that might support the discussion's rather strong conclusions. Yet such evidence can hardly be furnished, and it may be instructive to spell out the reasons.

EVIDENCE ABOUT DISCOVERY

Econometricians have endeavored to measure the consequences of particular economic policies. Much of their ingenuity and sophistication has been called forth to grapple with the formidable problem of describing *what might have occurred* in the absence of particular policies. The problem of describing concretely what might have happened but did not, it should be noted, exists even in situations in which all the alternatives before relevant decision makers are clearly defined, so that one at least knows the list of options from among which choices would have been forthcoming. The problem derives from the circumstance that it is not possible, without more or less sophisticated conjecture, to be confident as to which of an array of options a particular decision maker *might* have selected in hypothetical circumstances.

This problem becomes infinitely more formidable if one wishes to describe, in specified hypothetical circumstances, *what might have been spontaneously discovered.* Here the problem is not merely that a particular decision maker's preferences are unknown. The problem is that one cannot imagine what specific, now unknown opportunities might have been discovered in the relevant hypothetical circumstances.

One should not be surprised, therefore, that the losses from the regulatory stifling of market discovery processes are difficult to single out. Indeed, one should not be surprised that analysis, too, has tended to overlook such losses. Therefore one can only hope to draw brief attention to studies that perhaps can provide some illustrative flavor of the kinds of losses attributable to regulatory constraints, to which I have sought to direct attention. For purposes of such illustration, I draw on work focusing on the discovery process initiated by the lure of entrepreneurial profit in technological innovation and in corporate entrepreneurial endeavor.

DISCOVERERS: INNOVATORS

Much recent work by economists is devoted to gaining insight into the process of technological innovation. A small part of that work has considered the impact of government regulation on innovative activity at the technological frontiers. Although the authors of these studies are not primarily concerned with the impact of regulation upon entrepreneurial incentives, it is difficult to read their work without noticing its direct relevance to this essay's concerns.

A 1971 Brookings Institution volume, for example, was devoted to a symposium examining technological change in regulated industries (in particular electric power, telecommunications, and air and surface transportation).[34] In the analytical framework within which this examination was conducted, brief attention is paid to the thesis (attributed, perhaps too hastily, to Schumpeter) that it is "the incentive to earn very large profits" which "spurs entrepreneurs to introduce new techniques," so that the limits on possible profits imposed by regulatory commissions may inhibit such innovation.[35]

A similar possible link between regulatory constraints and the possible slowing down of the processes of technological discovery is noted particularly in the context of drug research in the pharmaceutical industry. The classic paper by Professor Peltzman, examining the impact of the 1962 drug amendments upon drug research, together with the work of others, has led to widespread discussion of the possibility that drug research in the United States lags seriously behind that of other countries.[36] Peltzman's results do not prove that regulation inhibits entrepreneurial discovery, which means the discovery of hitherto unknown opportunities, unknown even in the sense that it had not been known that they were there to be discovered. That is, Peltzman's findings would fit in equally well with a theory of search based on the assumption of awareness of discoverable opportunities waiting to be researched if the cost were not too high. Nonetheless, once attention is focused on entrepreneurial discovery, it is difficult to avoid linking Peltzman's results with the postulation of an entrepreneurial discovery process hampered by regulatory constraints.

DISCOVERERS: INSIDERS

Another important area in which the role of entrepreneurial discovery has been explicitly explored is that of decision making by corporate managers. In his definitive study of the issue, Henry Manne discusses the impact upon the exercise of entrepreneurship in the corporate firm of regulatory restrictions on insider trading.[37] Manne's study thoroughly examines the entrepreneurial role and its expression in a world of corporations. The study identifies the incentives of entrepreneurial profit needed to evoke the entrepreneurial role and the part that insider trading, in the absence of regulatory prohibition, might play to provide profit opportunities to reward entrepreneurial success. Restrictions on insider trading, Manne shows, no matter how plausible the motives underlying the regulatory restrictions may appear, tend to inhibit the exercise of entrepreneurship in corporate firms.[38]

Conclusion

This essay draws attention to some less obvious drawbacks of government regulation of the market. These drawbacks are rooted in the way regulatory restrictions, restraints, and controls interfere with the spontaneous discovery process that the unregulated market tends to generate. These drawbacks are also to be clearly distinguished from other disadvantages that flow from government intervention.

The peculiar character of the perils of regulation identified here closely parallels certain economic problems associated with the operation of the socialist economy. The review of the Mises-Hayek criticisms of the possibility of economic calculation under socialism provides a classic source for an Austrian perspective on the market process, and simultaneously the review provides important lessons for an understanding of the dangers inherent in regulation.

Recognition of these dangers can be most helpful in explaining the inefficiencies and the stagnation that appear so consistently to beset modern interventionist economies. It is in the nature of the subject, however, that the recognition of these perils does not lead easily to the provision of clear-cut examples of such regulatory damage. Nonetheless, in a modest way it is possible to illustrate these perils from contemporary discussions of palpable problems.

An emphasis on the perils of regulation that arises out of concern for the market process does not, in and of itself, justify the absolute condemnation of government regulation of the market process. Such condemnation would require full consideration, in addition, not only of other perils than those discussed here, but also of the hoped-for benefits sought through regulation of the market. Ultimately, public policy must depend on the value judgments of the policymakers or of those they wish to serve. But, no policy decisions with respect to government regulation can be properly arrived at without a full understanding of all the dangers inherent in such regulation. And such a full understanding arises particularly out of studying the market process of entrepreneurial discovery.

SEVEN

Entrepreneurship and the Future of Capitalism

All of us like to peer into the future. We are all curious to know now what we, or perhaps our grandchildren, eventually will see and experience. And not unnaturally, we look to the practitioners of our intellectual disciplines to help provide this desired prescience. If our thirst for informed future gazing is deep in respect to the physical universe, it is virtually unslakable in respect to the social and, particularly, the economic environments. We look to our social scientists, and in particular to our economists, to tell us what the future holds in store. Surely, we reason, if only we understood how the economic world works, we should be able to know now what the future outcome of economic processes is likely to be. And the more thoroughly and profoundly we understood these workings of the economic world, we assume, the better equipped we would feel ourselves to be to provide accurate and specific forecasts of future economic conditions, and the longer would be the future period for which we would believe our forcasting ability to hold scope.

I believe that my discussion of the role of entrepreneurship in the workings of the economic system will, in this sense, prove somewhat paradoxical. I shall in fact attempt to show that the future course of a capitalist economy does indeed depend crucially upon the present and future exercise of entrepreneurship. However, the more thoroughly and profoundly we understand the way en-

From *Entrepreneurship and the Outlook for America,* Jules Backman, ed. Copyright © 1983 by New York University. Reprinted with permission of The Free Press, a Division of Macmillan, Inc.

trepreneurship shapes and determines economic phenomena, the *less* well equipped we must recognize ourselves to be to make detailed forecasts of the shape of things to come. In fact, I shall argue, it is precisely this recognition of our inability to foresee the course of the future entrepreneurial process that constitutes a significant deepening of our understanding of the way the world works.

For an economics in which the role of entrepreneurship is not acknowledged (and it is now being admitted that much of received economic theory is guilty of just this failure), the possibilities for forecasting must appear much more promising. But the better we understand the manner in which entrepreneurial discoveries generate economic progress, the more humble we practitioners of economic science ought to become. This of course does not mean that our understanding of entrepreneurship actually weakens our ability to know the future accurately; rather, it reveals to us how arrogant and illusionary it would be (or was) for us ever to claim such accurate foreknowledge. Our appreciation for the entrepreneurial element will thus enable us indeed to understand the future course of capitalism more accurately than we could know it without such appreciation—but less accurately than we would, in our ignorance of entrepreneurship, have *thought* ourselves to be able to know it. Let us explore how an appreciation of entrepreneurship affects our understanding of the future of capitalism.

In the following pages two basic tools in the economist's kit are considered: the economist's notion of resource allocation and the economist's understanding of capitalism as a system of markets at or near equilibrium. I shall argue that, valuable and useful as these notions may be for many purposes, they prove inadequate and even downright misleading for any deeper understanding of the ongoing capitalist process. For such more sensitive understanding, we shall discover, it will be necessary to perceive how the exercise of entrepreneurship sharply

attenuates the importance of efficient resource allocation
and renders profoundly unhelpful an analytical perception of the capitalist system as being at or close to equilibrium. Moreover, it will turn out, the longer the future
period about which we are curious, the more serious and
damaging these limitations will prove to be.

The Allocation Paradigm

It is fifty years since Lionel (now Lord) Robbins
enunciated his definition of the scope of economics in
terms of the allocation of scarce resources among alternative goals.[1] Largely as a result of Robbins's brilliant
clarification of the issues, economists have learned to
focus their attention on the concept of *allocative efficiency*. In other words, economists ask whether, in view of
the given ranking of goals desired and the given array of
resources available, the operative decisions are such as to
ensure that no lower-ranked goal is attained at the ex-
pense of any more highly ranked goal. Where the allocation of resources has been in this sense inefficient, the
economist is prepared to discuss the importance of reallocating resources from the lesser valued to the more
highly valued goals.

Now there can be no doubt that Robbins's formulation has been enormously beneficial for economics. It
provided economics with an analytical framework that
has been extremely helpful in many ways. It directs the
attention of economists to the kinds of questions that, in
many contexts, are indeed precisely the questions that do
need to be answered. It enabled economists to recognize
that their theorems had generality extending far beyond
the narrow context of material wealth and welfare (to
which nineteenth-century economics had come to be
confined). Yet as we shall see, this allocation paradigm
has in certain ways proved something of a stumbling
block. *Economists have adopted the allocation criterion
with such enthusiasm as to apply it to contexts for which*

it has in fact no relevance. And particularly where they have indeed applied it in such illegitimate fashion, economists have become trapped in their own paradigm; they have failed to recognize crucial aspects of socioeconomic problems that simply do not fit into the allocation framework.

Thus, in many of our textbooks of elementary economics, undergraduates are taught that economics deals with the problem of how a nation or a society can solve "its economic problem," that is, how it can efficiently allocate "its" scarce resources among "its" competing goals.[2] But of course this involves an altogether questionable extension of Robbins's formulation. Robbins was concerned exclusively with *individual* economizing, or allocative, activity. He did not make the leap from the clear-cut allocation problem as it faces the individual to the altogether problematic notion of allocation with respect to a *society* of individuals. As Professor Buchanan has pointed out,[3] before one can talk sensibly about an allocation problem facing a society, it is first necessary to solve certain highly intractable and well-known difficulties that plague welfare economics. (Thus, unless one is prepared to make interpersonal comparisons of utility, it is not at all clear what one is to mean by the notion of a ranking of the importance *to society* of alternative production possibilities.)

More to the point, perhaps, of our specific concerns here is the circumstance that the allocation paradigm tends to divert attention away from the entrepreneurial function. The very problem that Robbins identified so clearly and so valuably is set up entirely in terms that presume a *given* framework of ends ranked and resources available. Before the economizing agent ever embarks on seeking the optimal allocative solution to the economizing problem, he is presumed to have already identified, somehow, the range of alternative courses of allocative action from among which he may choose. His economic problem, as defined by Robbins, does not encompass the task of *discovering* hitherto unnoticed available courses of action. (It is of course true that one of the *already given* courses of action available may be to undertake a systematic search along specified lines. But the notion of "given available courses of action" has no room for the step that *discovers*, say, that a systematic search may be a potentially useful course of action.) The problem of allocation presumes a given set of ranked goals—it does not consider the possibility of the discovery of additional goals that may be worthy of pursuit or of the discovery that some different ranking of these goals may be in fact desirable. The allocation paradigm presumes a perceived array of available means and a perceived array of technical formulas for the deployment of these means—it does not encompass the discovery of new resources available or the discovery of new technical uses to which they may be put.

In other words, the allocation paradigm, valuable though it is, bears the disadvantage of drawing analytical attention away from the entrepreneurial function of ensuring the continuing awareness of worthwhile goals, of not overlooking available means—of ensuring that desirable opportunities not be neglected by oversight. And serious enough as this disadvantage may be in respect to individual allocation, *it is of even greater potential harm in regard to the (illegitimate) extension of the allocation concept from the level of the individual to that of the society.* To talk of society allocating its resources presumes a given, perceived framework of scarce resources available to society. This way of discussing the economic problems facing society may permit analysis of how such given scarce resources can be optimally deployed, but it diverts attention away from those dimensions for economic activity along which there may occur entrepreneurial discovery of hitherto unanticipated stocks of resources or hitherto unglimpsed possibilities for the technological deployment of known resources. Clearly, the longer the prospective period we are contemplating, the more serious it becomes to overlook the implications of entrepreneurial escape from the instantaneous finity of resources. We shall return to these considerations after taking account of similar questions that should be raised about the second of the basic tools in the "economist's kit" mentioned earlier.

Capitalism and Market Equilibrium

This second tool is the vision of the capitalist economy adopted by mainstream economists which sees it as a system of markets at or near equilibrium. In this view, a free market (that is, pure capitalist) economy achieves fairly close conformity at all times to a configuration of prices which encourages sets of attempted purchases and sales of each input and of each produced consumer good— that can all be successfully carried out without regret and without disappointment. In other words, the activities undertaken by each market participant are such as to permit them all to be sustained. No one produces a commodity and finds it impossible to sell it at a price that justifies its costs of production. No one seeking a commodity with an eagerness financially justifying its production fails to find that it has been produced. All markets clear. All plans made are able to be carried out; no one subsequently regrets not having made a different plan. Or to put the matter somewhat differently, no one is, in the light of the going market prices, tempted to undertake plans that incorrectly anticipate the plans that others (inspired by the same market prices) are in fact making.

Here there can be no doubt that an understanding of the way markets work has, on the whole, been greatly helped by the insight that what occurs in markets is not random or haphazard but is the logical outcome of systematic forces which (if they could work themselves out in unimpeded fashion) can be imagined eventually to generate the above conditions of equilibrium. There is indeed no doubt that most of the market prices we observe have been powerfully affected, at least, by these systematic forces of market adjustment. For many purposes, especially where attention is focused on a small part of the market, it is an excusable simplification for analysis to proceed as if these forces of market adjustment have indeed already fully completed their tasks. Yet it must be pointed out that, to a very important extent, a view which sees the capitalist economy as a system of markets at or near equilibrium is not merely a *simplified* view of capitalism but also a *distorted* view. This view is distorted in perceiving, as the salient feature of capitalism, its being at all times close to the fully coordinated state—when in fact the salient feature of capitalism is surely to be found, rather, in the ceaseless market agitation generated by the continual discovery of *failures* in coordination. Of course it is this ceaseless agitation of the market which is responsible for the considerable coordinative properties which capitalism certainly possesses.

But a view of the market as a sequential, systematic process of continual adjustment, incessantly buffeted and redirected by exogenous changes, is one sharply at variance with the view of it as expressing at all times an approximately fully adjusted state of affairs. This difference is one that more recent critics of orthodox economics have not failed to identify. What is important, for present purposes, is for us to recognize that the responsibility for this distortion with which we have charged the standard, equilibrium view of capitalism rests with its failure to incorporate the entrepreneurial element into its perspective. As soon as entrepreneurial activity is permitted an essential role in the analysis of capitalism, the focus of attention shifts from already completed states of equilibrium to ongoing processes of adjustment and of responsive change.

The Role of Entrepreneurship in Capitalism

In the preceding sections we have observed that the incorporation of entrepreneurship into economic analysis sharply limits the usefulness of two important tools in the standard economist's tool kit. I wish, in this paper, to examine the implications of these observations for our ability to peer into the future course of a capitalist economy. Let us briefly review the meaning and role of entrepreneurship. For our purposes it will perhaps be excusable to set forth by assertion a number of insights and definitions developed more extensively (and less dogmatically) elsewhere.[4]

An individual decision maker exercises entrepreneurship in discovering opportunities for improving his circumstances that have hitherto not been known to him. Such entrepreneurial discovery is a matter not of correct calculation but of correctly perceiving the elements to be considered in performing calculation. In other words, entrepreneurial discovery consists not in achieving efficiency in dealing with a given situation but in alertness to the possibility that the true situation (with respect to which efficiency would be worth pursuing) is in fact different from the situation that had been assumed to be given. A significant aspect of the entrepreneurial dimension of individual decision making is that, along this dimension, the fixity of available resources is no longer absolute. Entrepreneurship consists, in part, in the discovery of hitherto unnoticed reserves of available resources.

In a capitalist economy, the scope for and exercise of individual entrepreneurship correspond, in significant degree, to characteristic features of the market process. Where a market has not yet attained equilibrium, this manifests itself in opportunities for individual entrepreneurial gain. The discovery and pursuit of such entrepreneurial profit constitute and drive the market process, during which such profit opportunities are ground down by entrepreneurial competition. We may distinguish two levels at which entrepreneurship may be exercised in a capitalist system.

First, at a given date a market economy is likely to be less than fully coordinated *with respect to information currently possessed.* Specific knowledge may at this moment exist in the minds of some market participants. Other market participants may, nonetheless, be engaged in activities that are imperfectly coordinated in light of the availability of this knowledge. Entrepreneurship may be exercised in harnessing this existing knowledge and in this way modifying the pattern of market activities. What the entrepreneur does, in this case, is discover the existence and/or the value of *available* knowledge.

The second level at which entrepreneurship may be exercised in the market is made possible by the circumstance that, at any given date, there presumably exist innumerable useful truths that *might* be known but which, at the moment, are unknown to *anyone* in the market. Entrepreneurship may thus be exercised not through the discovery of existing knowledge but in the discovery of totally new truths or, at least, in the discovery and anticipation of the prospective relative values of resources as they will be affected by future discovery of such new truths.

Both levels of entrepreneurship, it should be emphasized, constitute the discovery of hitherto incomplete coordination. At the first level, a market participant might, for example, be producing at high cost when technology currently available might permit production at much lower cost. The incompleteness of coordination, in such a case, may be illustrated very simply. Imagine two adjacent rooms in each of which a given item is being bought and sold. Because of the wall between the two rooms, participants in each of the two markets are, let us imagine, unaware of the existence of the market in the adjacent room. As a result the traded item sells for $10 in the first room and for $20 in the second. Clearly we have here incomplete coordination of buying and selling decisions. There are those in the first room who might be willing to sell if only the price were, perhaps, as high as $14. At the same time there are those in the second room who might be willing to buy if only the price were as low as $16.

Conditions for mutually beneficial trade between these parties clearly exist, yet they are not being applied.

This incomplete coordination with respect to *existing* information is a result of failure of market participants to exploit the arbitrage opportunity created by the difference in price between the two rooms. Entrepreneurship, in such cases, will then take the form of the discovery of this pure profit opportunity—thus driving prices together and eliminating the incomplete coordination that arose from the original imperfect mutual awareness on the part of market participants. The existence of currently available technology that could produce, at a cost of $10, an item selling for $20, represents precisely this kind of scope for entrepreneurship. There might be potential consumers for the item if only it could be produced and sold for less than $16. This possibility indeed exists yet is not being pursued. Producers have apparently not yet discovered that the technology *already* exists for such low-cost production. The entrepreneur who discovers the opportunity of buying all necessary inputs for $10 and selling the output for $20 is correcting the incompleteness of coordination with respect to *currently existing* knowledge.

At the second level, the incompleteness of coordination is of a different kind, but it exists nonetheless. Current market activities may be fully coordinated *with each other* yet be very imperfectly coordinated with future activities *as these will eventually turn out to be informed by as yet undiscovered truths.* The current price of natural gas and the current level of its consumption may be fully coordinated with one another and with other current prices and market activities (informed by the most up-to-date intelligence). Yet this price may be "too high" and consumption "too low" from the perspective (that may, in several years, be provided by technological or other discoveries) of the possibilities, say, of tapping solar energy. Today these possibilities simply do not exist; yet entrepreneurship may be exercised in anticipating their discovery. Entrepreneurial gain here is captured by anticipating price changes in the future that would never emerge simply on the basis of information existing today.

It should thus be observed that at both of these two levels at which we have identified entrepreneurial activity, such activity may be described as making up an equilibrating and coordinating tendency. At the first level, where imperfect coordination existed with respect to existing information, entrepreneurship may be seen as steering present prices and present decisions in the direction of the relevant, coordinated equilibrium configuration. At the second level, where entrepreneurship consists in arriving at or in anticipating wholly novel truths, it may be seen as tending to coordinate present decisions with future decisions and present prices with future prices; entrepreneurship, at this second level, may be seen as nudging the system in the direction of intertemporal equilibrium. But there is an important difference between these two senses on which the entrepreneurial market process "achieves a tendency towards equilibration."

Entrepreneurship, Equilibration, and the Determinacy of the Future

The central theorem of economics, the theorem which permits economists to view market phenomena as the understandable outcome of systematic forces rather than as a random sequence of events, is what demonstrates the equilibrative and coordinative tendencies in the market process. It is this theorem which permits us to feel confident that, sooner or later, a tendency will have asserted itself toward the social integration of all the currently available information scattered throughout the economy.[5]

So it is the entrepreneurial market process which justifies, to some extent, the view that society as a whole tends to achieve a coordinated balance among the innumerable activities of its individual members, *in a manner analogous to the way we view—à la Robbins—each individual as achieving allocative efficiency with respect to the given goals and resources relevant to that individual.* From this perspective the scarcity of resources, including information, available to society, together with the arrays of preferences displayed by the individual members of society, tends to "determine" the allocation of resources within the economy in a manner analogous to that in which each individual's budget allocations are seen as "determined" by his preference rankings and the array of resources available to him. So it is the fixity and scarcity of existing societal resources that is, in part, the source of whatever "determinacy" economic science enables us to perceive in observed market phenomena.

Now this presents us with a certain paradox. We saw earlier that it is our recognition of the entrepreneurial element that limited, in my view, the significance of the concept of efficient resource allocation (which serves for many economists as the central theme of their discipline). In addition I questioned the possibility of applying the concept of allocative efficiency to a society as a whole, arguing that the concept as expounded by Lord Robbins was one that had reference strictly to individual choice. Yet, as indicated in the preceding paragraph, economic analysis does surely demonstrate the tendency toward the achievement of coordination within a society, at least analogously to the coordination achieved by the efficiently allocating individual economizer. And, paradoxically, it is precisely the operation of the entrepreneurial element (the recognition of which *limited* for us the significance of the allocation concept) that provides some justification for the treatment of society as a whole as achieving a balanced allocation of resources.

The discussion in the preceding section can throw further light on these matters: in exactly the same way that the recognition of the entrepreneurial element in individual action limits the relevance of the concept of individual allocative efficiency, we shall see that the recognition of the second level of those previously discussed, at which entrepreneurship is exercised in a market economy, limits the sense in which the economic achievements of a market can be grasped in terms—even as metaphor—of allocative efficiency. Let me try to clarify what by now must appear to be a somewhat confusing picture; I offer several summary observations.

1. Entrepreneurship as exercised through the market is responsible for its equilibrative and coordinative tendencies. While the ceaseless *operation* of entrepreneurially driven market forces underscores the inadequacy of the view of the market as at all times at or near equilibrium, nonetheless it is the results achieved by these forces that constitute whatever "allocative balance" a society may be thought to possess.

2. This "allocative balance" achieved in a market consists in reality, as Hayek showed, of the social integration of the innumerable scraps of existing information that are present in scattered form throughout society. The degree of social integration thus entrepreneurially achieved is what justifies, to a limited extent, the metaphorical treatment of an economic society as analogous to the Robbinsian allocating, economizing individual.

3. Yet the same entrepreneurial spirit that stimulates the discovery in the market of the value of information *now* existing throughout the market also tends to stimulate the discovery or "creation" of *entirely new* information concerning ways to anticipate or to satisfy consumer preferences. The entrepreneurial process at this second level is what drives the capitalist system toward higher and higher standards of achievement (quite apart from the economic progress, resulting from the systematic accumulation of invested capital, that is fully consistent with the coordination of *existing* information).

4. While, in a special sense, this progress in the capitalist economy arising from the entrepreneurial discovery or creation of totally new information may also be described as coordinative, nonetheless it represents an

escape from the limits imposed by the finite and scattered information possessed at earlier dates. In other words, in the context of this "long-run" entrepreneurial progress of the capitalist system, the metaphor of society as analogous to the Robbinsian economizing individual can no longer be sustained at all. The entrepreneurial discovery by an individual of new goals to pursue and new availability of resources cannot be subsumed under the allocative, maximizing model of individual decision making. In precisely the same way, the progress achieved by a capitalist system as a result of entrepreneurial discovery of totally new social opportunities renders totally inoperative the metaphor of the market as an efficient allocator of resources within the constraints of existing, limited resources.

At the outset of this chapter I announced my intention to show that recognition of the entrepreneurial element in capitalism would make it less and less possible for us to correctly anticipate specific information regarding capitalism's future course. We can now see why this must be so. Whatever limited determinacy may be ascribed to the market economy derives from the market's equilibrative propensities. To the extent that the market integrates existing scattered information concerning wants, technology, and available resources, it may be argued that the market's future course is determined by that existing stock of information. But to the extent that the market can, through long-run entrepreneurial discovery, transcend the limits of any existing constraints of knowledge, its future course becomes wholly indeterminate. We may argue, with great confidence, that under capitalism entrepreneurial discovery will disclose new arrays of social opportunities—but precisely because these are wholly new opportunities *created* by entrepreneurial discovery, they cannot be seen in any sense as the *inevitable* outcome of the entrepreneurial process. Our confidence in the creativity of entrepreneurship does not in any way suggest a determinate pattern in such creativity.

Technological Advance and Entrepreneurial Discovery

I should perhaps pause to emphasize that the long-run entrepreneurial process upon which I have rested my thesis for the future of capitalism is *not* quite the same process as is usually associated with technological advance. It is certainly often recognized that the long-run capacity of a capitalist system depends crucially on the rate of technological advance. As long ago as 1871 Carl Menger, founder of the Austrian School of Economics, wrote:

> The quantities of consumption goods at human disposal are limited only by the extent of human knowledge of the causal connections between things, and by the extent of human control over these things. . . . Nothing is more certain than that the degree of economic progress of mankind will still, in future epochs, be commensurate with the degree of progress of human knowledge.[6]

It would be possible to concur with Menger's prediction and yet argue that this prediction can be accepted within an "allocation" framework. That is, it would be possible to see advances in technological knowledge as the results of deliberate investment in search activity undertaken entirely within the perceived possibilities available at each date. Investment in R&D may, on this view, be seen as merely a special kind of investment that does not require us to transcend the "maximizing" model for an understanding of market outcomes.

The view advanced here is much closer, in this respect, to that of Schumpeter, who was thoroughly persuaded, of course, of the critical and creative role of entrepreneurship in capitalist development. In his vision, entrepreneurial activity is continually keeping "the capitalist engine in motion" through "the new consumers' goods, the new methods of production or transportation, the new markets, the new forms of industrial organization that capitalist enterprise creates."[7] This activity continually "revolutionizes the economic structure *from within* . . . destroying the old one . . . creating a new one. This process of Creative Destruction is the essential fact about capitalism."[8]

What I wish to emphasize is that this entrepreneurial process, because it cannot be captured within a Robbinsian maximizing framework—even one explicitly arranged to consider maximizing and allocation within a prospective multiperiod framework—is *in principle* beyond the scope of detailed prediction. But this does not mean we have nothing to say about the general character of this entrepreneurial process that so defies detailed prediction.

Entrepreneurship and the Future of Capitalism

The position I desire to convey can perhaps best be articulated by comparing it with that of a new book just published (1981) by Princeton University Press. In this book, *The Ultimate Resource*, its economist-author, Professor Julian L. Simon, adopts a provocatively unorthodox stance with respect to the likelihood of increasing resource scarcity and economic difficulties in the long-run future. Contrary to the prevalent view that "we are entering an age of scarcity in which our finite natural resources are running out, that our environment is becoming more polluted, and that population growth threatens our civilization and our very lives,"[9] Simon maintains vigorously that:

> [The] standard of living has risen along with the size of the world's population since the beginning of recorded time. And with increases in income and population have come less severe shortages, lower costs, and an increased availability of resources, including a cleaner environment and greater access to natural rec-

reation areas. . . . Contrary to common rhe-
toric, there are no meaningful limits to the
continuation of this process. . . . There is no
physical or economic reason why human resourcefulness and enterprise cannot forever
continue to respond to impending shortages
and existing problems with new expedients
that, after an adjustment period, leave us better
off than before the problem arose.[10]

Simon's theme parallels my own in certain respects,
although it is couched in different terminology. Yet certain differences between the two themes should perhaps
be pointed out. As I have argued, Simon maintains that
for long-run purposes economic resources should not be
treated as finite. "We see the resource system as being as
unlimited as the number of thoughts a person might
have."[11] The "ultimate resource" for Simon is "people—
skilled, spirited, and hopeful people who will exert their
wills and imaginations for their own benefit, and so, inevitably, for the benefit of us all."[12] A number of the optimistic observations made by Simon, for example,
concerning food supplies and population growth, are
strongly reminiscent of Schumpeter's spirited debunking
forty years ago of the stagnationist thesis.[13] (Somewhat
surprisingly, Simon appears not to refer to Schumpeter
throughout his book.) Simon's message, although
couched in different terms, parallels my own: the notion
of society's being constrained in scarce, given resources,
as is the individual in the Robbinsian framework, is not a
useful idea in predicting long-run trends in capitalism.

But whereas in my own treatment of this theme I
have placed great emphasis upon the notion of *entrepreneurship,* Simon nowhere, as far as I can discover, uses
this term in his discussions. Simon appears to rest his
case for optimism upon his analysis of past economic performance and upon his general faith in the imagination
and resourcefulness of human beings. Moreover, Simon's
confidence in these respects is so great as to lead him to

make specific, highly optimistic forecasts.[14] My own grounds for challenging the premise of long-run finiteness of resources has been more cautious and depends heavily on the scope permitted by the institutional environment for the free exercise of entrepreneurship.

Whereas Simon appears not to pay much attention to the institutional environment in which his forecasts are to have relevance, my own discussion points very much to the crucial importance of a capitalist framework. In the simplest sense of the term, of course, entrepreneurship—free enterprise—has scope only under free market capitalism. So the possibility of escaping from the long-run constraints of scarce resources through a series of horizon-expanding discoveries would appear to require a capitalist environment. Yet, on the other hand, it might be argued that in the broad sense of the term the concept of entrepreneurship is not necessarily confined to capitalism; after all, central planners may exercise entrepreneurial imagination, creativity, and discovery for the benefit of the socialized society. For my purposes here, it is not strictly necessary to comment on the scope for entrepreneurial discovery in a planned society; but several brief observations are in order insofar as the issue relates to the future of capitalism.

I have argued elsewhere[15] that the scope for entrepreneurship cannot, in general, be disengaged *from the prospect of winning entrepreneurial gain.* For a hitherto unperceived opportunity to be noticed by a potential entrepreneur, it is of great importance that the potential entrepreneur believe that any opportunity he perceives will somehow redound to his own benefit. This line of argument tends, of course, to point to the importance, within capitalism, of freedom of entry into markets and of untrammeled opportunity to gain from entrepreneurial opportunities perceived.

The relationship between entrepreneurship and the future of capitalism is thus a two-sided one. Only a capitalism in which freedom to grasp opportunities perceived is available to the fullest extent can encourage the fullest flowering of entrepreneurial discovery and creativity. On the other hand, it is the exercise of such long-run entrepreneurial creativity and discovery that permits us to see the economic system as liberated from the scarcity constraints that would compress us into an allocation framework.

We are not able to chart the future of capitalism in any specificity. Our reason for this incapability is precisely that which assures us (if not quite on the same grounds as Simon or with the same degree of specificity of optimism) the economic future of capitalism will be one of progress and advance. The circumstance that precludes our viewing the future of capitalism as a determinate one is the very circumstance in which, with entrepreneurship at work, we are no longer confined by any scarcity framework. It is therefore the very absence of this element of determinacy and predictability that, paradoxically, permits us to feel confidence in the long-run vitality and progress of the economy under capitalism.

Notes

Chapter One

1. See my "Classical Economics and the Entrepreneurial Role," in Israel M. Kirzner, *Perception, Opportunity, and Profit* (Chicago: University of Chicago Press, 1979).

2. For a survey and bibliography on theories of entrepreneurship during this period see F. H. Knight, *Risk, Uncertainty and Profit* (Boston: Houghton Mifflin, 1921), chap. 2.

3. W. J. Baumol, "Entrepreneurship in Economic Theory," *American Economic Review* 58 (May 1968): 64.

4. Robert F. Hébert and Albert N. Link, *The Entrepreneur: Mainstream Views and Radical Critiques* (New York: Praeger, 1982).

5. See Hébert and Link, *Entrepreneur.*

6. My earlier discussion on entrepreneurial alertness is contained in Israel M. Kirzner, *Competition and Entrepreneurship* (Chicago: University of Chicago Press, 1973) and Kirzner *Perception, Opportunity, and Profit.* See also Israel M. Kirzner, ed, *Method, Process and Austrian Economics: Essays in Honor of Ludwig von Mises* (Lexington, Mass.: D. C. Heath, 1982), chap. 12.

7. T. W. Schultz, "The Value of the Ability to Deal with Disequilibria," *Journal of Economic Literature* 13, 3 (September 1975): 827–46.

8. G. L. S. Shackle, *Epistemics and Economics: A Critique of Economic Doctrines* (Cambridge: Cambridge University Press, 1972), p. 364.

9. These sections owe much to Roger W. Garrison, "Austrian Economics as the Middle Ground," in *Method, Process, and Austrian Economics,* ed. Israel M. Kirzner (Lexington, Mass.: Lexington Books, 1982). Garrison's work was highly commended in G. L. S. Shackle, "Decisions, Process and the Market," *Journal of Economic Studies* 10, 3 (1983): 61.

10. See F. A. Hayek, "Economics and Knowledge," *Economica* 4 (February 1937): 33–54, reprinted in Hayek, *Individualism and Economic Order* (London: Routledge and Kegan

Paul, 1949), for an early discussion of processes of equilibration treated as being processes of learning.

Chapter Two

1. That is, the problem of achieving maximum desirable results without overstepping the constraints imposed by the limited resources available. This emphasis on maximization is to be traced to the influence of Lionel H. Robbins, *The Nature and Significance of Economic Science* (London: Macmillan, 1932).

2. The literature on the economics of search proceeds on this basis. The classic article is G. J. Stigler, "The Economics of Information," *Journal of Political Economy* 69 (June 1961): 213–25.

3. An elaboration of this theme is in my *Competition and Entrepreneurship* (Chicago: University of Chicago Press, 1973), chaps. 1–3.

4. F. H. Knight, *Risk, Uncertainty and Profit* (Boston: Houghton Mifflin, 1921).

5. A fuller discussion of this insight is in my *Perception, Opportunity, and Profit* (Chicago: University of Chicago Press, 1979), chaps. 9, 10.

6. In Ludwig von Mises, *Human Action* (New Haven: Yale University Press, 1949), p. 253.

7. A complete discussion of this central theorem of welfare economics is in W. J. Baumol, *Economic Theory and Operations Analysis*, 4th ed. (Englewood Cliffs, N.J.: Prentice-Hall, 1977), chap. 21.

8. F. A. Hayek, "Competition as a Discovery Procedure," in *New Studies in Philosophy, Politics, Economics and the History of Ideas* (Chicago: University of Chicago Press, 1978).

9. Oskar Lange, "On the Economic Theory of Socialism," in Oskar Lange and Fred M. Taylor, *The Economic Theory of Socialism*, ed. Benjamin E. Lippincott (New York: McGraw-Hill, 1964), p. 70. The initial statement by Mises demonstrating the problems in socialist economic calculation was "Die Wirtschaftsrechnung im sozialistischen Gemeinwesen," *Archiv für Sozialwissenschaften und Sozialpolitik* 47 (April 1920): 86–121, reprinted in *Collectivist Economic Planning*, trans. and ed. Friedrich A. Hayek (London: Routledge and Kegan Paul, 1935). Hayek's own response to Lange is contained in his *Individualism and Economic Order* (London: Routledge and Kegan Paul, 1949).

10. Joseph S. Berliner, *The Innovation Decision in Soviet Industry* (Cambridge: MIT Press, 1976).

11. Further discussion of this theme is in my "The Perils of Regulation: A Market-Process Approach," Occasional Paper of the Law and Economics Center, University of Miami, 1978, reprinted in this volume, chap. 6.

Chapter Three

1. L. von Mises, *Human Action* (New Haven: Yale University Press, 1949), p. 253.

2. Ibid., p. 288.

3. Ibid., p. 255.

4. Ibid., p. 254.

5. Ibid., p. 105.

6. Israel M. Kirzner, *Competition and Entrepreneurship* (Chicago: University of Chicago Press, 1973), pp. 86–87.

7. Ibid., chap. 2. See also Israel M. Kirzner, *Perception, Opportunity, and Profit* (Chicago: University of Chicago Press, 1979), chap. 10.

8. F. A. Hayek, *Individualism and Economic Order* (London: Routledge and Kegan Paul, 1949), p. 42.

9. Kirzner, *Competition and Entrepreneurship*, pp. 86–87 (italics in original).

10. Such activity was subsumed under arbitrage by pointing out the formal similarity between (1) buying and selling in different markets today and (2) buying and selling in different markets at different dates (see Kirzner, *Competition and Entrepreneurship*, pp. 85–86).

11. Henry Hazlitt, review of *Competition and Entrepreneurship*, in *Freeman* 24 (December 1974): 759. Similar concerns seem to be expressed in a review of *Competition and Entrepreneurship* by Percy L. Greaves, Jr., in *Wertfrei* no. 2 (Spring 1974), esp. pp. 18–19.

12. See unpublished paper by Murray N. Rothbard, "Professor Hébert on Entrepreneurship," pp. 1–2. Quoted with permission.

13. Ibid., p. 7.

14. L. H. White, "Entrepreneurship, Imagination, and the Question of Equilibrium," unpublished paper (1976). See also L. H. White, "Entrepreneurial Price Adjustment" (paper presented at Southern Economic Association meetings, Washington, D.C., November 1978), p. 36, n. 3.

15. J. High, review article on *Perception, Opportunity, and Profit* in *Austrian Economics Newsletter* 2, 3 (Spring 1980): 14.

16. High's criticisms of my references to uncertainty as a characteristic of the entrepreneurial environment focus most specifically on what he believes to be my use of uncertainty to

"serve as the distinguishing characteristic between entrepreneurship and luck" (ibid.). Here there seems to be a definite misunderstanding of my position. Far from the presence of the uncertainty surrounding entrepreneurship being what separates entrepreneurial profit from the lucky windfall, almost the exact reverse is the case. What marks entrepreneurial profit as different from the lucky windfall is that the former was, despite the (inevitable) uncertainty that might have discouraged the entrepreneur, in fact deliberately pursued. Where luck confers gain it may well reflect the circumstance that the uncertainty of this gain deterred the actor from even dreaming of winning it. High's reading apparently resulted from his understanding a passage that he cites (from Kirzner, *Perception, Opportunity, and Profit*, pp. 159–60) to represent the case of a purely lucky gain. In fact the passage cited does not refer to luck at all. If one knows that one's labor can convert low-valued leisure into high-valued apples, the apples one so gains through one's hard work do not constitute a lucky windfall. The point of the cited passages is that Menger's law shows there is no value gain at all derived from that labor, since one would already have attached the higher value of the ends to the available means. My discussion in this chapter, however, proceeds on the assumption that High's unhappiness at my treatment of uncertainty in entrepreneurship does not rest solely on the validity of the way I distinguish entrepreneurial profits from windfall gains.

17. Mises, *Human Action*, p. 253.

18. See Kirzner, *Competition and Entrepreneurship*, pp. 32–35. See also Kirzner, *Perception, Opportunity, and Profit*, pp. 166–68.

19. G. L. S. Shackle, *Epistemics and Economics* (Cambridge: Cambridge University Press, 1972), p. 136 (italics in original).

20. Ibid., p. 351.

21. See also Israel M. Kirzner, *The Economic Point of View* (Princeton: Van Nostrand, 1960), p. 167.

22. See also Kirzner, *Perception, Opportunity, and Profit*, chap. 9.

23. F. H. Knight, *Risk, Uncertainty and Profit* (New York: Houghton Mifflin, 1921), p. 268.

24. Mises, *Human Action*, p. 105.

25. See Kirzner, *Perception, Opportunity, and Profit*, chap. 10, esp. pp. 158–64.

26. Ibid., p. 162.

27. Ibid., p. 163.

28. See, for example, Kirzner, *Competition and Entrepreneurship*, p. 39.

29. See note 15 of this chapter.

30. B. J. Loasby, *Choice, Complexity and Ignorance* (Cambridge: Cambridge University Press, 1976), p. 5.

31. Knight, *Risk, Uncertainty and Profit*, p. 199.

32. Our discussion proceeds in terms of the market for a single commodity. It could be couched, without altering the essentials in any respect, in more general terms. See also the subsequent section of this chapter.

33. The three pairs of statements may be viewed as additions to the two lists of twelve statements developing the analogy between the individual and the market provided in Kirzner, *Perception, Opportunity, and Profit*, chap. 10, pp. 170–72, 173–75.

34. J. A. Schumpeter, *The Theory of Economic Development* (Cambridge: Harvard University, 1934), p. 137; J. A. Schumpeter, *History of Economic Analysis* (Oxford: Oxford University, 1954), p. 556. See also S. M. Kanbur, "A Note on Risk Taking, Entrepreneurship and Schumpeter," *History of Political Economy* 12 (Winter 1980): 489–98.

35. J. B. Clark, "Insurance and Business Profit," *Quarterly Journal of Economics* 7 (October 1892): 46 (cited in Knight, *Risk, Uncertainty and Profit*, p. 38).

36. Shackle, *Epistemics and Economics*, p. 122.

37. White, "Entrepreneurship, Imagination," p. 7.

38. L. M. Lachmann, "From Mises to Shackle: An Essay," *Journal of Economic Literature* 14 (March 1976): 59.

Chapter Four

1. J. A. Schumpeter, *Theorie der wirtschaftlichen Entwicklung* (Leipzig, 1912); English translation, *Theory of Economic Development* (Cambridge: Harvard University Press, 1934). See also Schumpeter, *Capitalism, Socialism and Democracy* (New York: Harper and Row, 1942).

2. Harvey Leibenstein, *General X-Efficiency Theory and Economic Development* (New York: Oxford University Press, 1978), p. 9.

3. See the statement by Joan Robinson, *Economic Journal* 73 (March 1963): 125: "The strong case for the price mechanism lies in the allocation of scarce resources between competing uses. . . . But no one has ever been able to make out a case (on grounds of economic efficiency) for *laissez-faire* in the sphere of investment." See also Israel M. Kirzner, "On the Premises of Growth Economics," *New Individualist Review* 3, 1 (Summer 1963): 20–28.

4. See also Israel M. Kirzner, "Entrepreneurship and the Future of Capitalism," in *Entrepreneurship and the Outlook for*

America, ed. J. Backman (New York: Free Press, 1983), reprinted in this volume, chap. 7.

5. L. H. Robbins, *Nature and Significance of Economic Science*, 2d ed. (London: Macmillan, 1935).

6. G. L. S. Shackle, *Epistemics and Economics* (Cambridge: Cambridge University Press, 1972).

7. Israel M. Kirzner, "Hayek, Knowledge, and Market Processes," in *Perception, Opportunity, and Profit* (Chicago: University of Chicago Press, 1979).

8. Israel M. Kirzner, "Uncertainty, Discovery and Human Action: A Study of the Entrepreneurial Profile in the Misesian System," in *Method, Process, and Austrian Economics: Essays in Honor of Ludwig von Mises*, ed. Israel M. Kirzner (Lexington, Mass.: D. C. Heath, 1982), reprinted in this volume, chap. 3.

9. This and the succeeding sections of this chapter draw on my approach to understanding the role of the entrepreneur as developed in earlier works, especially *Competition and Entrepreneurship* (Chicago: University of Chicago Press, 1973) and *Perception, Opportunity, and Profit* (Chicago: University of Chicago Press, 1979).

10. See Kirzner, *Competition and Entrepreneurship*, pp. 97 ff. See also, D. T. Armentano, *Antitrust and Monopoly: Anatomy of a Policy Failure* (New York: Wiley, 1982), chaps. 1 and 2.

11. F. A. Hayek, *The Road to Serfdom* (Chicago: University of Chicago Press, 1944).

12. Kirzner, "Entrepreneurship and the Future of Capitalism," p. 161.

13. A. Seldon, "Preface," in Kirzner et al., *The Prime Mover of Progress: The Entrepreneur in Capitalism and Socialism*, ed. A. Seldon (London: Institute of Economic Affairs, 1980), pp. xi–xii.

14. R. F. Hébert and A. N. Link, *The Entrepreneur: Mainstream Views and Radical Critiques* (New York: Praeger, 1982), p. 11.

15. B. Gilad, "On Encouraging Entrepreneurship: An Interdisciplinary Approach," *Journal of Behavioral Economics* 11 (Summer 1982): 132–63.

16. See, for example, K. de Schweinitz, "Free Enterprise in a Growth World," *Southern Economic Journal* 29 (October 1962): 103–10.

17. See also N. Balabkins and A. Aizsilnieks, *Entrepreneur in a Small Country* (Hicksville, N.Y.: Exposition Press, 1975), chap. 10; A. V. Bruno and T. T. Tyebjee, "The Environment for Entrepreneurship," in *Encyclopedia of Entrepreneurship*, ed. C.

A. Kent, D. L. Sexton, and K. H. Vesper (Englewood Cliffs, N.J.: Prentice-Hall, 1982).

18. A. Seldon, "Preface," p. xvi.

Chapter Five

1. Ludwig von Mises, *Human Action* (New Haven: Yale University Press, 1949), p. 253.

2. My critical discussion here of Professor Shackle's position pertains only to the one paper cited (first published in 1949). I certainly do not wish to suggest that that paper adequately represents the comprehensive view on pure profit developed by Professor Shackle in the course of a number of later works.

3. G. L. S. Shackle, *Expectations in Economics* (Cambridge: Cambridge University Press, 1952), p. 96.

4. Ibid., pp. 95–96.

5. Ibid., p. 99.

6. See Shackle, *Expectations in Economics*, pp. 73n, 96.

7. On this see the doctoral dissertation, B. Gilad, "An Interdisciplinary Approach to Entrepreneurship: Locus of Control and Alertness" (New York University, 1981).

8. It should be noted in this respect that, since *other* courses of action do not involve this riskiness, the incentive needed to render this risky course of action preferred must be of "the first kind."

9. See the dissertation cited in note 7.

10. Joan Robinson, *Economic Philosophy* (Harmondsworth, Middlesex: Penguin Books, 1962), p. 57.

11. For more discussion of the "finders-keepers ethic" and its relevance for entrepreneurial profit, see Israel M. Kirzner, *Perception, Opportunity, and Profit* (Chicago: University of Chicago Press, 1973), chaps. 11 and 12.

12. I am indebted to Professor L. M. Lachmann for drawing my attention to this classification.

13. See Henry G. Manne, *Insider Trading and the Stock Market* (New York: Free Press, 1966).

Chapter Six

1. For the literature on private incentives for public regulation, see George J. Stigler, "The Theory of Economic Regulation," *Bell Journal of Economics and Management Science* 2 (Spring 1971): 3–21; reprinted in Stigler, *The Citizen and the State* (Chicago: University of Chicago Press, 1975); Richard A. Posner, "Theories of Economic Regulation," *Bell Journal of Economics and Management Science* 5 (Autumn 1974): 335–58;

Sam Peltzman, "Toward a More General Theory of Regulation," *Journal of Law and Economics* 19 (August 1976): 211–40.

2. The most trenchant recent criticisms of government regulation from this perspective include Ludwig von Mises, *Human Action* (New Haven: Yale University Press, 1949), part 6; Milton Friedman, *Capitalism and Freedom* (Chicago: University of Chicago Press, 1962); Friedman, *An Economist's Protest* (Glen Ridge, N.J.: Thomas Horton and Daughters, 1972).

3. Ludwig von Mises, "Die Wirtschaftsrechnung im sozialistischen Gemeinwesen," *Archiv für Sozialwissenschaften und Sozialpolitik* 47 (April 1920): 86–121; reprinted in *Collectivist Economic Planning*, trans. and ed. Friedrich A. Hayek (London: Routledge and Kegan Paul, 1935).

4. Ludwig von Mises, *Socialism: An Economic and Sociological Analysis*, trans. J. Kahane (New Haven: Yale University Press, 1951), part 2, sect. 1; this edition is translated from the second German edition (published 1932) of Mises's *Die Gemeinwirtschaft* (originally published in 1922); see also Mises, *Human Action*, part 5.

5. Hayek, *Collectivist Economic Planning*.

6. Friedrich A. Hayek, "Socialist Calculation: The Competitive 'Solution,'" *Economica* 7 (May 1940): 125–49; reprinted as "Socialist Calculation III: The Competitive 'Solution,'" in Hayek, *Individualism and Economic Order* (London: Routledge and Kegan Paul, 1949).

7. Oskar Lange, "On the Economic Theory of Socialism," in Oskar Lange and Fred M. Taylor, *On the Economic Theory of Socialism*, ed. Benjamin E. Lippincot (New York: McGraw-Hill, 1964).

8. Trygve J. B. Hoff, *Economic Calculation in the Socialist Society*; trans. M. A. Michael (London and Edinburgh: Hodge, 1949).

9. Dominic T. Armentano, "Resource Allocation Problems under Socialism," in *Theory of Economic Systems: Capitalism, Socialism, Corporatism*, ed. William P. Snavely (Columbus, Ohio: Merrill, 1969), pp. 133–34.

10. Hayek, "Socialist Calculation III." Reviewed particularly were Lange, "On the Economic Theory of Socialism," and Henry D. Dickinson, *Economics of Socialism* (London: Oxford University Press, 1939).

11. Thus they agreed with Mises and Hayek that efficiency is impossible without indicators of value and that any hope of solving the problem by direct mathematical methods (for example, by solving the Walrasian equation system) is illusory.

12. Hayek, *Individualism and Economic Order*, p. 187.

13. Abba P. Lerner, *The Economics of Control* (New York: Macmillan, 1944).

14. See most recently Murray N. Rothbard, "Ludwig von Mises and Economic Calculation under Socialism," in *Economics of Ludwig von Mises*, ed. Laurence S. Moss (Kansas City: Sheed and Ward, 1976).

15. Lange, "On the Economic Theory of Socialism," p. 70.

16. Ibid., pp. 70–71.

17. This assumption, of course, is vulnerable to serious question. See James M. Buchanan, *Cost and Choice* (Chicago: Markham, 1969), chap. 6; G. Warren Nutter, "Markets without Property: A Grand Illusion," in *Money, the Market, and the State: Essays in Honor of James Muir Waller*, ed. Nicholas A. Beadles and L. Aubrey Drewry, Jr. (Athens: University of Georgia Press, 1968). It is important to note that the argument stated in the text does *not* depend on any doubt concerning managers' ability and motivation to obey rules. Were socialist managers to be given price lists, then we may assume for the purposes of the present discussion that they *could* make decisions *as if* they were intent on maximizing "profits." (Of course, the profits maximized in equilibrium contexts are not pure entrepreneurial profits. This distinction is discussed later in this essay.)

18. Lange, "On the Economic Theory of Socialism," p. 65–72.

19. Particularly in Mises, *Human Action*, chap. 15.

20. Hayek, "Economics and Knowledge," "The Use of Knowledge in Society," and "The Meaning of Competition," all reprinted in *Individualism and Economic Order*. In this respect the work of Austrian-born Joseph A. Schumpeter is of considerable relevance for the Austrian view of the market; see particularly Schumpeter, *The Theory of Economic Development*, trans. Redvers Opie (New York: Oxford University Press, 1961); this work first appeared in German in 1912 and was first translated by Opie in 1934. See also Schumpeter, *Capitalism, Socialism and Democracy* (New York: Harper and Row, 1950), chap. 7.

21. This section draws freely from my *Competition and Entrepreneurship* (Chicago: University of Chicago Press, 1973), and *Perception, Opportunity, and Profit* (Chicago: University of Chicago Press, 1979).

22. Friedrich A. Hayek, ed., "Competition as a Discovery Procedure," in *New Studies in Philosophy, Politics, Economics and the History of Ideas* (Chicago: University of Chicago Press, 1978).

23. See Hayek, "Economics and Knowledge," "The Use of Knowledge in Society," and "The Meaning of Competition."

24. See Kirzner, *Perception, Opportunity, and Profit,* chaps. 2, 8, 9.

25. Once again, we assume away criticisms based on the view that regulation may be motivated not by the wish to benefit consumers, but by the wish to benefit the regulators and those they regulate.

26. While these considerations support a stance critical of regulation, in and of themselves they do not necessarily declare regulation to be wrong, or even inefficient. Given sufficiently strong value judgments on the part of would-be regulators—whether in favor of environmental purity, of an egalitarian distribution of wealth, of freedom from pornography or disease, of national prestige, of the enrichment of the arts, or of whatever—criticism of intervention, from the perspective of these value judgments, may (properly) carry little weight. The economist's task, however, is to spell out as fully as possible the consequences of alternative policies, so that policy decisions at least will not be taken on the basis of erroneous assessments of their likely consequences. The discussion in the following pages does not offer an airtight case against intervention but draws attention to possibly grave perils of intervention, perils that seem to have been taken fully and explicitly into account neither by the literature critical of interventionist policies nor, a fortiori, by the uncritical proponents and supporters of government regulation.

27. Here an improvement in the allocation of resources (given the initial pattern of resource distribution) is defined as a change in the pattern of input utilization and/or input consumption that improves the well-being of each member of the economy. Although this definition is close to the norm of Paretian welfare economics, it does *not* invoke the notion of aggregate welfare.

28. "The Austrian finds no detailed explanation in welfare economics of how government is supposed to obtain the information necessary to carry out its assigned tasks. The knowledge required . . . is not to be found collected in one place, but rather dispersed throughout the many members of the economy." Stephen C. Littlechild, *The Fallacy of the Mixed Economy: An "Austrian" Critique of Economic Thinking and Policy* (London: Institute of Economic Affairs, 1978), p. 40. See also Gordon Tullock, *The Politics of Bureaucracy* (Washington, D.C.: Public Affairs Press, 1965), p. 124: "Administrative problems . . . could . . . be of such complexity that the centralization of information necessary to make decisions effectively in a bureaucracy might not be possible."

29. It is even most cogently pointed out that the very notion of cost, seen from the perspective of the regulator, is unlikely to coincide with any notion of cost that one might wish to consider relevant to the quest for efficiency. See Buchanan, *Cost and Choice*, chaps. 5 and 6.

30. Professor Machlup valuably refers to the "fertility of freedom" in generating discovery of new possibilities. Fritz Machlup, "Liberalism and the Choice of Freedoms," in *Roads to Freedom: Essays in Honour of Friedrich A. von Hayek*, ed. Erich Streissler (London: Routledge and Kegan Paul, 1969), p. 130.

31. Murray L. Weidenbaum, "The Impact of Government Regulation" (study prepared for the Joint Economic Committee, Subcommittee on Economic Growth and Stabilization, United States Congress, July 1978). See also Ernest C. Pasour, "Hide and Seek: Hidden Costs of Government Regulation," *World Research INK* 2 (December 1978): 5.

32. "There is ample evidence that imagination and innovation are not stilled by restrictive legislation—only diverted to figuring out ways around it." Freidman, *Economist's Protest*, p. 149.

33. See, for example, Nicholas Sanchez and Alan R. Waters, "Controlling Corruption in Africa and Latin America," in *The Economics of Property Rights*, ed. Eirik Furubotn and Svetozar Pejovich (Cambridge, Mass.: Ballinger, 1974); Edward C. Banfield, "Corruption as a Feature of Governmental Organization," *Journal of Law and Economics* 18 (December 1975): 587–605; and Simon Rottenberg, "Comment," *Journal of Law and Economics* 18 (December 1975): 611–15.

34. William M. Capron et al., eds., *Technological Change in Regulated Industries* (Washington, D.C.: Brookings Institution, 1971).

35. Ibid., p. 8. See also chap. 2.

36. Sam Peltzman, "An Evaluation of Consumer Protection Legislation: The 1962 Drug Amendments," *Journal of Political Economy* 81 (September–October 1973): 1049–91. See also David Schwartzman, *Innovation in the Pharmaceutical Industry* (Baltimore: Johns Hopkins Press, 1976).

37. Henry G. Manne, *Insider Trading and the Stock Market* (New York: Free Press, 1966).

38. Although there are many other studies illustrating the hidden distortions generated by regulation, I do not cite them here, since they do not obviously call our attention to the market discovery process and its modification as a result of the regulatory constraints.

Chapter Seven

1. See Lionel Robbins, *An Essay on the Nature and Significance of Economic Science,* 2d ed. (London: Macmillan, 1935), pp. 12–16.

2. For examples see W. J. Baumol and A. S. Blinder, *Economics, Principles, and Policy* (New York: Harcourt Brace Jovanovich, 1979), p. 45.

3. J. M. Buchanan, *What Should Economists Do?* (Indianapolis: Liberty Press, 1979), pp. 20–22.

4. See Israel M. Kirzner, *Competition and Entrepreneurship* (Chicago: University of Chicago Press, 1973), and idem, *Perception, Opportunity, and Profit:* (Chicago: University of Chicago Press, 1979).

5. Cf. F. A. Hayek, "The Use of Knowledge in Society," *American Economic Review* 35, 4 (September 1945): 519–30; reprinted in *Individualism and Economic Order* (London: Routledge and Kegan Paul, 1949).

6. Carl Menger, *Principles of Economics* (1871; translated by J. Dingwall and B. Hoselitz, 1950; New York: New York University Press, 1981), p. 74.

7. J. A. Schumpeter, *Capitalism, Socialism, and Democracy,* 3d ed. (New York: Harper and Row, 1950), p. 83.

8. Ibid.

9. Julian L. Simon, *The Ultimate Resource* (Princeton: Princeton University Press, 1981), p. 15.

10. Ibid., p. 345.

11. Ibid., p. 347.

12. Ibid., p. 348.

13. Schumpeter, *Capitalism, Socialism, and Democracy,* chap. 10.

14. See Simon, *Ultimate Resource,* pp. 21, 27.

15. Israel M. Kirzner, "The Perils of Regulation: A Market-Process Approach," Occasional Paper of the Law and Economics Center University of Miami, 1978, reprinted in this volume, chap. 6; idem, "The Primacy of Entrepreneurial Discovery," in Israel M. Kirzner et al., *The Prime Mover of Progress: The Entrepreneur in Capitalism and Socialism,* ed. A. Seldon (London: Institute of Economic Affairs, 1980), reprinted in this volume, chap. 2.

Index

Aizsilnieks, A., 174
Alertness. *See* Entrepreneurial
  alertness
Arbitrage. *See* Entrepreneurship
Armentano, Dominick T., 124,
  174, 176
Austrian approach to economics,
  67, 126, 129, 164, 178

Balabkins, Nicholas, 174
Banfield, Edward C., 179
Bastiat, F., 121
Baumol, William J., 169, 170, 180
Berliner, Joseph S., 170
Blinder, A. S., 180
Bruno, A. V., 174
Buchanan, James, 153, 177, 180

Cantillon, Richard, 1
Capitalism: future of, 150–68;
  market, ix; as process of cre-
  ative discovery, ix
Capron, William M., 179
Certainty, model of, 18
Choice, 47. *See also* Decisions;
  Economizing, Robbinsian;
  Human action
Clark, John B., 65, 173
Classical economists, 1
Competition, dynamic, 87, 130
Counter-expected, distinct from
  unexpected, 106–9

Decisions: and deliberation, 47–
  48; and entrepreneurial element, 16, 45–56; and

Robbinsian maximization, 16,
  51. *See also* Human action
de Schweinitz, K., 174
Dickinson, H. D., 125
Discovery, x, 78, 93–118, 130;
  taxation of, 111–14. *See also*
  Entrepreneurial discovery;
  Search

Economic growth, 68–92
Economic problem, 15, 87, 153
Economizing, Robbinsian, 45, 81,
  153, 170
Ends-means framework, adoption
  of, 46
Entrepreneur, neoclassical view
  of, 8
Entrepreneurial: activities, 6;
  alertness, 7, 10–13, 22, 56, 63,
  85, 89–91; attitudes, stimulation of, 90; creativity, 7, 56,
  63–64; discovery, 11, 15–39,
  87–89; error, 19; function, distinct, 1; hunch, 22;
  imagination, 44, 104–5; incentives for, 26, 28, 57–61, 86;
  judgment, 43; process, x, 68–
  92; profit, 57, 91; role, disap-
  pearance in economics, 3; role,
  reappearance in economics, 5;
  role, in Walras, 3
Entrepreneurship: and arbitrage,
  63, 84, 116; cannot be hired,
  27; coordinative function of,
  60–61, 87–88; as costless, 24,
  89; danger of taking for granted,

181